BETWEEN
THE
TESTAMENTS

Other books by Charles F. Pfeiffer

THE DEAD SEA SCROLLS
THE BOOK OF GENESIS
THE BOOK OF LEVITICUS

BETWEEN THE
TESTAMENTS

Charles F. Pfeiffer

BAKER BOOK HOUSE
Grand Rapids, Michigan

CONTENTS

Preface

part one

The Persian
Period

part two

The Hellenistic
Period

PREFACE

The time between the close of Old Testament history and the beginning of the New Testament period has often been called "the four hundred silent years." To the historian, however, these centuries were anything but silent, and they seem to become more vocal with each passing decade.

To the student of ancient history, names like Cyrus, Darius, and Alexander the Great make this period one of paramount importance. The Jew notes during these centuries the development of synagogue worship, the successful Maccabean revolt, and the emergence of those parties within Judaism which have set the pattern for Jewish life and thought during the past two millennia.

The Christian looks upon the Old Testament as preparatory, looking toward the fulfillment of its hopes and promises in the Person of Jesus Christ. He is interested in the history of the centuries preceding the coming of Christ, for he sees in them a preparation for the advent, and a progress toward that period of history termed "the fulness of time" (Gal. 4:4).

The Dead Sea Scrolls have done much to quicken an interest in the literature of the Jews during the inter-Testament period. It is the purpose of this brief volume to outline the broader background necessary for the appraisal of those movements which immediately precede the advent of the Savior.

part one

**The Persian
Period**

1

CYRUS, AND THE RISE OF THE EMPIRE

I. The Beginnings

The Persian Empire came into being as the result of the efforts of one man — Cyrus. Of his background we know nothing. His father was named Cambyses, and the ancestry of his mother is unknown. Tradition makes her the daughter of a Median king. The story was probably invented to make Cyrus appear as a legitimate monarch of royal Median ancestry.

Cyrus first appears in history when, in 559 B.C., at the age of forty, he inherited the small kingdom of Anshan. This territory was tributary to the Median Empire, one of the eastern rivals of Babylon.

The Medes and the Babylonians were former allies. In 612 B.C. their combined forces destroyed Nineveh, the capital of the Assyrian Empire. Kyaxeres the Mede seems to have taken the lead in the assault on Nineveh. Nabopolassar of Babylon, however, fought the Assyrians alone after the destruction of their capital city. Perhaps the Medes were called home by problems that required immediate attention. Median and Babylonian leaders may have become estranged as a result of a conflict of interests. In any event, the Medo-Babylonian alliance was short-lived. The fall of Nineveh and the subsequent end of Assyria brought about a realignment of the states of the ancient Near East.

Babylon quickly capitalized on Assyria's disaster. Nebuchadnezzar, son of Nabopolassar and commander of the Babylonian armies, marched westward and annexed the territories which had once belonged to Assyria. Egypt tried to make trouble for Nebuchadnezzar, with a view to the annexation of additional territory, but the tide of Babylonian victory could not be stopped.

All this also affected the Jews. The last kings of Judah were
torn between the claims of Egypt and Babylon. Jeremiah had
insisted that resistance to Nebuchadnezzar was futile, and the
pro-Egyptian party succeeded in bringing about a series of rebellions. The result was tragic. By 587 B.C. Nebuchadnezzar had
destroyed Jerusalem, with its Temple. Most of the Judeans were
taken to Babylon.

Exile in Babylon brought the Jews to a fresh realization of
the nature of their God. Idolatry had been rampant during the
years before the fall of Jerusalem. The exile was seen as punishment for this unfaithfulness to Yahweh, the God of Israel. With
the destruction of the Temple, animal sacrifices ceased. In place
of the Temple, synagogues became the accepted houses of worship. There the sacred *Torah* was read and explained. It comprised the first five books of the Bible, the pentateuch. The
word "Torah" is usually translated "law," but might better be
rendered "instruction." The *Torah* gave instruction by example
as well as by precept. Ultimately other sacred books were accepted as inspired Scripture. Jeremiah was lightly dismissed during the years of his ministry in Jerusalem, but in Babylonian
exile his countrymen came to see that his prophecies were true.
A collection of the "Prophets" — including some of our historical
books — came into being. The Synagogue also recognized a third
section of the Old Testament, the "Writings," beginning with
the Book of Psalms and including books of poetry as well as
history and prophecy. The New Testament bears testimony to
the Law, the Prophets, and the Psalms as the three sections of
Scripture. This threefold division is still used in printed edi-
tions of the Hebrew Bible.

When Cyrus came to the throne of Anshan, Nabonidus
(Nabu-naid) was the unpopular king in Babylon. A philosopher and mystic, he felt called by Marduk to restore the temple of the moon-god Sin at Harran. When Nabu-naid protested
that the proximity of the Medes would prevent the enterprise,
Marduk, through his priests, replied:

"The Mede of whom you are speaking, he himself, his land, and the
kings who march at his side are not! When the third year comes, the
gods will cause Cyrus, king of Anshan, his little slave, to advance
against him with his small army. He will overthrow the wide extending
Medes; he will capture Astyages, king of the Medes, and take him captive
to his land."[1]

Had Marduk been a true prophet he might have added that
Babylon would soon fall into the hands of Cyrus also.

1. Abu Habba Cylinder, col. 1, 11. 8-32. Quoted in A. T. Olmstead, *History
of the Persian Empire*, p. 36.

In 550-549 B.C. Cyrus revolted against Astyages, his Median overlord. Meanwhile Nabonidus turned the kingship of Babylon over to his eldest son Bel-shar-usur (Belshazzar of the Book of Daniel) and headed for Harran, confident that the Medes had trouble enough with Cyrus to keep them busy. Such proved to be the case. Astyages sent an army under Harpagus against Cyrus, but Harpagus, remembering how Astyages had cruelly slain his son, deserted with most of his soldiers to Cyrus. Then Astyages determined personally to lead a second army against Cyrus. Reaching Parsa, the capital of Anshan, this second army mutinied against Astyages and handed him over to Cyrus.

Cyrus proved to be a generous conqueror. Although he did not hesitate to plunder the wealth of Ecbatana, the Median capital, the city itself was spared and became one of the capitals of the Medo-Persian Empire. Many of the Median officials were kept at their posts. This policy of clemency was new in the politics of the Near East, but it was to characterize the reign of Cyrus.

With the conquest of Media, Cyrus fell heir to Median claims in Assyria, Mesopotamia, Syria, Armenia, and Cappadocia. Some of these claims conflicted with those of Babylon, and we read no more of an alliance between Babylon and Cyrus. Beside the Medo-Persian Empire there were now three great powers — Lydia, Babylonia, and Egypt. The first two of these were subdued by Cyrus himself. His son Cambyses was to conquer the third.

2. Cyrus and Lydia

The Kingdom of Lydia first enters history when, in 660 B.C., Ashurbanipal demanded tribute of a Lydian king "Gyges of Luddi." The kingdom of Lydia was the country lying west of the Halys River in Asia Minor. It was blessed with fertile land and natural resources, not the least of which was gold. Gyges had conquered an area known as the Troad, giving his people an outlet to the sea. Under the fifty-seven year reign of Alyattes, grandson of Gyges, Lydia became a major power. Alyattes took Smyrna, the greatest port on the Asia Minor coast and, one by one, added the Greek coastal towns to his domain. Benevolent in his rule, Alyattes permitted the Greek cities to retain their own customs, institutions, and local government. Their taxes, however, helped the Lydian monarch to become the richest ruler of his age.

Croesus, the son and heir of Alyattes, completed the capture of the Greek settlements on or near the Aegean Sea by adding Ephesus and Miletus to his empire. His fabulous wealth is responsible for the simile, "as rich as Croesus." Herodotus repeats a legend to the effect that Solon visited Croesus and instructed him in the meaning of life by a series of illustrations summarized in the phrase, "Call no man happy until he is dead."

After the conquest of the Medes, the outer fringes of Cyrus' empire reached the eastern bank of the Halys River. Sooner or later a showdown must come with Lydia.

Cilicia offered no resistance when Cyrus laid claim to his provinces in Asia Minor. Realizing the imminence of attack, Croesus, however, hastily made alliances with Amasis, king of Egypt, and Nabu-naid of Babylon. Sparta offered him her fleet. Cyrus determined to strike immediately when he learned of Croesus' action through Eurybatos, a trusted friend of Croesus who betrayed his country. Eurybatos had been entrusted with large sums of money to be used in raising mercenaries in the Peloponnesus. Instead he fled to Cyrus and informed him of the plans of Croesus.

Leaving Sardis, Croesus crossed the Halys River for his first encounter with Cyrus. He consulted the oracles. They told him that, if he should send an army against the Persians, he would destroy a great empire. They had failed to tell him which empire! Croesus' initial victories over the Cappadocians filled him with confidence. When Cyrus offered Croesus his throne and kingdom in exchange for recognizing Persian sovereignty, Croesus was in no mood to accept. He indignantly retorted that he had never been subject to another power, whereas the Persians had been slaves to the Medes and would be the future slaves of the Lydians. Cyrus attacked at once.

After two indecisive battles, Croesus was driven from the field in a hopeless rout. He felt sure that Cyrus would not pursue him to Sardis because of the cold, snowy season which was approaching. Cyrus determined, however, not to wait until the allies of Croesus could come to his aid. Herodotus tells of the decisive battle in which camels were placed in the Persian front line to face the famed cavalry of Croesus. The horses, which had never seen camels before, stampeded. The infantry was unable to rally, and the battle became a rout, with the broken forces of Croesus seeking refuge in Sardis.

Although Croesus sent pleas for aid to Egypt, Greece, and Babylon, it was too late to save the day. The Spartans hastened to prepare their fleet, but before it could be launched, word arrived that Sardis had fallen and Croesus was a prisoner of the Persians.

The Nabu-naid Chronicle gives this official report of Cyrus: "In the month Aiaru (May) he marched against the country Lydia . . . killed its king, took his possessions, put (there) a garrison of his own."[2] Legends suggest that Cyrus dealt kindly with Croesus, allowing him to live in comfort near the ancient capital of Media. Actually it appears that Croesus followed the oriental custom of immolating himself to escape the usual indignities heaped upon a captured monarch before he was put to death. An Attic vase painter, Myson, within a half century of the death of Croesus, depicted him enthroned upon a pyre which a servant was about to light.

The once wealthy Lydian Empire now became the Persian satrapy of Saparda, or Sardis. A native Lydian, Pactyas, was placed in charge of the captured treasure of Croesus.

3.   Cyrus and the Greeks

The conquest of Lydia brought Cyrus into contact with the Greek cities of Asia Minor which had made their peace with Croesus. Cyrus demanded that the coastal cities recognize his sovereignty, but they refused, only to be conquered one by one by the might of Persian arms or the diplomacy of Persian gold. There were Greeks, however, who welcomed Cyrus. The city of Miletus was shrewd enough to realize that Cyrus held the future, and submitted to him.

For some reason, the priests of Apollo, the Greek god of oracles, were thoroughly sympathetic with Cyrus. It was Apollo of Delphi who had uttered the ambiguous oracle that lured Croesus to his death. Apollo of Miletus, through his priests, was also clearly sympathetic with the Persians. When the city of Cyme asked counsel of the Apollo oracle concerning the disposal of a Greek who had rebelled against the Persians, Apollo ordered the surrender of the Greek rebel.

With the conquest of Greek Asia Minor, two Persian satrapys were formed. The Ionian satrapy was joined to Sardis, and the area south of the Hellespont was organized into a satrapy named "Those of the Sea."

Sooner or later Persia would have to fight the mainland Greeks. The Persians learned much from their dealings with the Greek cities of Asia Minor. Other important conquests in the

2. Translation of A. Leo Oppenheim in James B. Pritchard, ed., *Ancient Near Eastern Texts*, p. 306.

East must precede a final showdown with the Greeks, however.

4. Cyrus Heads Eastward

While Cyrus was conquering Lydia and Greek Asia Minor, Nabonidus was having his own troubles in Babylon. Under Nebuchadnezzar, Babylon had developed into a progressive and efficient state. Graft and mismanagement which developed under Nabonidus and his son Belshazzar brought on conditions of near starvation. Gobryas, or Gubaru as the Babylonians called him, had been one of Nebuchadnezzar's ablest generals. To him was entrusted the governorship of the Babylonian province of Elam, or Gutium. To add to the woes of Nabonidus, Gobryas deserted to Cyrus and began to attack Babylonian territory. His first blows were directed against the ancient city of Uruk, the Erech of Genesis 10.

Meanwhile Cyrus was giving his attention to the less civilized but strategically important lands to the east. While the wealth of his empire came from the west, for security reasons Cyrus had to control the east. The lands of Hyrcania and Parthia had been united before Cyrus had turned eastward. Their *kavi*, or local kinglet, was Hystaspes, famous as the father of Darius the Great. Hystaspes acknowledged the sovereignty of Cyrus and continued his rule as a Persian satrap.

The details of Cyrus' eastern campaign were not chronicled, as were those of his conquests of Lydia and Babylon. We know, however, that Cyrus continued his eastward march, incorporating Dragiana, Arachosia, Margiana, and Bactria into his empire. He crossed the Oxus River and reached the Jaxartus, where he built fortified towns to defend his northeastern frontier against the attacks of central Asian nomads.

5. The Fall of Babylon

Cyrus next turned his attention to Babylon. In this expedition he considered himself the deliverer rather than the conqueror of Babylon, and this feeling was shared by many Babylonians. The priests of Marduk, the god of Babylon, were happy to welcome Cyrus.

There was good reason for dissatisfaction with Nabonidus. He was an archaeologist and a mystic at heart. Like the famous Pharaoh Akhnaton of Egypt, Nabonidus was wholly unsuited by temperament for the office of ruler. An incompetent may succeed for a time if his challengers are equally incompetent, but Nabonidus was faced with the genius of a Cyrus. There was a time when Cyrus might have been stopped. Croesus might have succeeded in checking him had Babylon acted swiftly to aid her northern ally. But Nabonidus was spending his time in Teima watching the excavation of temple sites and admiring the handiwork of his predecessors. No aid reached Croesus, and Cyrus marched on.

Nabonidus was a very religious man. He chose to let the gods act as his guardians. When Babylon was threatened, he imported images of the gods from the surrounding cities, but this only added to dissatisfaction. The custodians of these local shrines were unhappy to have their temples plundered. The priests of Marduk in Babylon felt neglected, because Nabonidus seemed preoccupied with a host of "foreign" deities. Nabonidus alone lived in a fools' paradise.

In early October, 539 B.C., Cyrus was ready to invade lower Mesopotamia. Since the defenses of Babylon were reputedly impregnable, Cyrus had wisely bypassed Babylon until he had secured the territory to the east and to the west of the fabulous city. When Cyrus arrived, however, he was able to advance unchecked.

After an initial encounter at Opis, Sippar was taken without battle on October 11th. Nabonidus fled from Babylon, leaving his son Belshazzar in charge. Two days later, Gobryas, the governor of Elam (Darius of Daniel 6), captured Babylon without battle. Belshazzar was slain. Gobryas was named satrap of the new province of Babirush by Cyrus, who personally entered Babylon later in the month and proclaimed peace to everyone in the city.

The Cyrus Cylinder gives Cyrus' own account of the capture of Babylon:

> "Marduk, the Great Lord, a protector of his people / worshipers, beheld with pleasure his [i.e. Cyrus'] good deeds and his upright mind [lit.: heart] [and therefore] ordered him to march against his city Babylon. He made him set out on the road to Babylon going at his side like a real friend. His widespread troops — their number, like that of the water of a river, could not be established, could not be established — strolled along, their weapons packed away. Without any battle, he made him enter his town Babylon, sparing Babylon any calamity."[3]

Cyrus realized the value and the need of a "return to normalcy" in Babylonian affairs. The reign of Nabonidus had been abnormal, but Marduk himself had provided a righteous ruler in the person of Cyrus. This is the way Cyrus himself describes it: "Marduk . . . scanned and looked [through] all the countries, searching for a righteous ruler . . . he pronounced the name of

3. Cyrus Cylinder, Pritchard, *op. cit.*, p. 315.

Cyrus, king of Anshan, declared him to be [come] the ruler of all the world."[4]

The disapproval of the priests of Marduk had been a major factor in the downfall of Nabonidus. Cyrus showed his co-operation with the Babylonian priests by going through the prescribed ritual at the great New Year Festival. By taking the hand of the god of Babylon he legalized the new line of Babylonian kings. Cyrus became "king of Babylon, king of the land."

Cyrus also determined to restore to their own shrines the gods which had been taken to Babylon by Nabonidus. The Cyrus Cylinder declares this as a matter of policy: "Furthermore, I re-settled upon the command of Marduk, the great lord, all the gods of Sumer and Akkad whom Nabonidus has brought into Babylon to the anger of the lord of the gods, unharmed, in their [former] chapels, the places which make them happy."[5]

The Babylonians had made it a practice to remove peoples from their homeland and settle them under the watchful eyes of the Babylonian kings. Such a policy had been used by Assyria. Assyria not only moved populations from their former homes, but moved others in to occupy the vacated areas. The ancestors of the Biblical Samaritans had such a history (II Kings 17:23-24, see also Chapter VII).

The Assyrian policy of permanent transportation meant the end of any hope for return to its former territory by the members of the exiled northern tribes. The Babylonians had not re-settled the Jerusalem area, however, and the exiles beside the waters of Babylon continued to weep as they remembered Zion. They longed for return to the land of their fathers.

Such restorations were part of the "back to normalcy" policy of Cyrus. Of the captive peoples he writes: "I [also] gathered all their [former] inhabitants and returned [to them] their habitations."[6]

The motives of Cyrus may not have been entirely humanitarian. Egypt was on the agenda, and thoroughly loyal settlers in the buffer area of Syria-Palestine would be of great help when Persia undertook the conquest of Egypt. Cyrus was wise as well as humane, and his policy with respect to captive peoples exhibited both aspects of his character.

6. Cyrus and the Jews

When Cyrus became lord of Babylonia, the dependencies of

4. *Ibid.*
5. *Ibid.* p. 316.
6. *Ibid.*

Babylon likewise came under his control. He adopted a benevolent policy toward those former Babylonian provinces on the principle that the happier their lot, the more likely they would be to co-operate with Persian aims and goals. Phoenicia pledged its loyalty and its fleet, which was the match of any the united Greeks could raise.

The policy of the restoration of captive deities and captive peoples had special application to the Jews, whose religious ideals were respected by Cyrus and his successors as superior to those of the other nations with whom they dealt. To be sure, the Jews had no image that must be restored to its shrine, but Nebuchadnezzar had taken utensils from the Temple at Jerusalem. They had been used in Belshazzar's feast. If the gods of the other nations were restored, certainly the vessels used in the worship of the God of Israel must receive similar treatment.

Many Jews had prospered in Babylon and had no desire to leave. Not only were they permitted to remain, but many of them prospered in business and government during the Persian period. Daniel was among those that remained. The Book of Esther records both the influence and the trials of Jews in the Persian Empire. Nehemiah was cupbearer to a Persian king.

Yet the prophetic predictions of a return to a glorious Zion were not wholly unheeded. The permission to return for the purpose of rebuilding the Temple was made the subject of an official decree:

> "As for the house of God which is at Jerusalem, Let the house be built, the place where they offer fire continually; its height shall be ninety feet and its breadth ninety feet, with three courses of great stones and one of timber. And let its cost be given from the king's house. Also, let the gold and silver utensils of the house of God, which Nebuchadnezzar took from the house of God and brought to Babylon, be restored and brought again to the Temple which is in Jerusalem, each to its place. And you shall put them in the house of God" (Ezra 6:3-5).

The utensils were taken from Esagila, the temple of Babylon, and entrusted to a Jewish prince who had been appointed governor of Judah, Sheshbazzar (perhaps Shamash-apal-usur) by name. About 50,000 Jews availed themselves of the opportunity to return to their fatherland with the blessing and help of Cyrus. Aside from the assertion in Ezra 5:16 that he "laid the foundation of the house of God which is in Jerusalem" in 537 B.C., we read no more of the activity of Sheshbazzar.

The leadership of the band of returned exiles passed to Zerubbabel *(Zer-babili,* "seed of Babylon") and Jeshua (or Joshua) the priest. Consonant with the edict of Cyrus, they built the

Altar of Burnt Offerings and began the offering of daily morning and evening sacrifices (Ezra 3:3). In the second year of their return the foundations of the Temple were laid amid scenes of great rejoicing (Ezra 3:12). Nothing more was accomplished in the work of rebuilding the Temple during the lifetime of Cyrus (Ezra 4:5).

The joyful enthusiasm of the early days of the return gave way to the gloomy frustration which resulted from the activities of "the adversaries of Judah and Benjamin" (Ezra 4:1). Northern Palestine was populated with the deported captives from the Assyrian conquests to whom the name Samaritan was given (see Chapter VII). In the Judean highlands, the Negev, and in southern Judah as far north as Hebron, the Edomites, or Idumeans, had settled. The Nabatean Arabs had pressed from the Arabian desert into the area that had been occupied by the Edomites from Patriarchal times. North of the Edomites, people known as the Calebites occupied the territory up to Bethlehem (I Chron. 2:50 ff.) These nations had profited from the expulsion of Judah in the days of Nebuchadnezzar. They could not be expected to hail the returning pilgrims with any enthusiasm.

To be sure, some of those, called "the adversaries of Judah and Benjamin," offered to co-operate in the task of rebuilding, alleging that they had been worshipers of the God of Israel, since they had been introduced to the land of Israel as a result of one of Esarhaddon's deportations (Ezra 4:2). They seem to have shared the common concept that each land has its own god and that, as settlers in Israel, they must worship the God of that land. The leaders in Israel were not convinced of the purity of their faith and replied bluntly: "You have no part with us in building an house unto our God. We ourselves, together, will build unto Yahweh, God of Israel, as King Cyrus, the king of Persia, has commanded us" (Ezra 4:3).

The "people of the land" used every conceivable tactic to hinder the Jews from their work of rebuilding the Temple. However, the power of the Persian Empire seems to have restrained the "adversaries of Judah and Benjamin" from a policy of open war. Ezra tells us that the adversaries "troubled them in building" and tried to persuade the Persian court that the rebuilding of Jerusalem would prove detrimental to Persian interests (Ezra 4:5, 11-16). The adversaries were temporarily successful. For a period of about eighteen years little or no progress was made in the rebuilding process. In the meantime Cyrus died and Cambyses and Darius succeeded to the throne of the Empire.

7. The Last Days of Cyrus

After the conquest of Babylon, Egypt alone remained of the allies of Croesus who had challenged Cyrus in his bid for world power. Plans for a campaign against Egypt were entrusted to Cyrus' son, Cambyses, while Cyrus personally set out to deal with a revolt of the nomads on the eastern frontiers of the empire. There, in what should have been a mere skirmish, Cyrus was wounded. In the steppe country east of the Caspian Sea he died. His body was carried back to Pasargadae, one of his capital cities.[7] There his body was covered with wax, according to Persian custom, and placed in a stately, dignified tomb which was guarded by faithful priests for two centuries. The tomb is still standing, but its contents have long since been removed.

Few world conquerors have been regarded as highly as Cyrus. The Persians called him father. The Greeks regarded him as a master and lawgiver. When Alexander the Great found that Cyrus' tomb had been rifled, he ordered that the body be replaced and the contents of the tomb be restored as far as possible. To the Jews he was the Lord's anointed who ended the Babylonian exile and opened a new era in the history of Israel. Cyrus did not force Persian ideas on his subjects, but rather formed a synthesis of the ancient cultures of Mesopotamia, Syria, Asia Minor, the Greek cities, and parts of India.

---

7. The others: Ecbatana, Babylon, and Susa.

2

CAMBYSES, AND THE CONQUEST OF EGYPT

For eight years before the death of Cyrus, his eldest son Cambyses had lived in Babylon and acted as his father's representative at the annual New Year's festival. A document dated February 20, 535 B.C., gives us a clue concerning the nature of his administration. Reference is made to the house of Nabu-mar-sharri-usur, steward of the King's Son. The name means "May Nabu protect the King's Son," and refers to Belshazzar, son of Nabonidus. The name suggests that its possessor was a palace dignitary, responsible for the welfare of members of the royal family. It is significant that Cambyses not only retained the civil officers of the Nabonidus regime, but kept the palace dignitaries as well.[1]

Persian custom decreed that the king should not leave his empire unprotected when he left for a foreign war. Before leaving to defend his eastern borders, Cyrus recognized Cambyses as regent with authority to use the title "King of Babylon." When news of his father's death reached Cambyses, he assumed his father's full title, "King of Babylon, King of Lands."

A second son, Bardiya, or Smerdis as the Greeks call him, was entrusted with the eastern provinces of the Empire. When the news of Cyrus' death reached the Empire, disorders broke out on all sides. These have commonly been attributed to an attempt of Bardiya to challenge Cambyses' right to the throne. The period is obscure, and the facts that have reached us have been interpreted differently. Cambyses is reported to have murdered his brother, concealing his death. Later, however, on his return from Egypt, Cambyses was to learn of the revolt of one who called himself Bardiya (known as Pseudo-Smerdis by the Greeks). The Behistun inscription (see Chapter III, sec. 2) of

---

1. A. T. Olmstead, *The History of the Persian Empire*, p. 87.

Darius agrees with the tradition that Cambyses actually murdered Bardiya:

> "He who was named Cambyses, the son of Cyrus, one of our race was king before me. That Cambyses had a brother, Bardiya by name, of the same mother and father as Cambyses. Afterwards Cambyses slew this Bardiya. When Cambyses slew Bardiya it was not known unto the people that Bardiya was slain."[2]

With the question of succession settled, Cambyses was free to proceed with the long-planned expedition against Egypt. The era of Egypt's greatness was long past, but her Pharaohs still had illusions of grandeur. Pharaoh Hophra had contested Nebuchadnezzar's claim to Palestine and encouraged Zedekiah to revolt. Trusting in Egyptian aid, Zedekiah defied Nebuchadnezzar. When Jerusalem fell in 587 B.C., the prestige of Egypt reached a new low.

Repercussions at home were hardly favorable to Hophra. A revolt among the warrior class was quelled by the skill of Amasis, a man who had come up through the ranks and held their confidence. Amasis was actually hailed as king, but a compromise was effected and a co-regency established in which Amasis had full power. Differences between Amasis and Hophra led to war and the death of Hophra. He was accorded a royal burial, but Amasis was free to go on with his own plans.

Seeing the rise of Cyrus and the Persian army, Amasis realized that he needed powerful friends. When the temple of Delphi was destroyed by fire in 548 B.C., he made a substantial contribution toward its rebuilding. He made an alliance with Polycrates, tyrant of Samos. The Greek world was the one hope of Amasis in his determination to challenge the Persian Empire. This alliance, however, was as much a disappointment to Egypt as Egypt had been to Judah in the contest with Nebuchadnezzar.

In about four years after his accession, having settled his domestic problems, Cambyses was ready to turn toward Egypt. While he halted at Gaza to survey the problems of marching his troops through the deserts and marshes which separated him from Egypt, unexpected help came. Polycrates of Samos decided to desert Amasis. In this way one of the best Greek generals in the service of the Pharaoh came to Cambyses to reveal the secrets of the Egyptian defense. This general, Phanes of Halicarnassus, put Cambyses in touch with the Sheikh of the Bedouin who arranged to station relays of camels with water

---

2. The Behistun Inscription, col. 1, line 10. Olmstead considers this account a fiction devised by the usurper Darius to legitimize his own rule. *Op. cit.*, p. 107 f.

along the route of march! The fifty-five miles of desert were quickly traversed, and Cambyses approached the walls of Pelusium where the Greek mercenaries were commanded by a son of Amasis, Psammeticus III. Amasis did not live to meet the attack of Cambyses. He died after a short illness. This seemed to be another ill omen to the already pressed Egyptians. A few days after the accession of Psammeticus III, rain fell at Thebes — a rare event which added to the nervous fear of the Egyptians.

After a fierce battle at Pelusium, Psammeticus and his armies fled to Memphis. Eighty years after the battle of Pelusium, Herodotus was shown the bones of the dead strewn over the battlefield.[3] He was told that Egyptian skulls were harder than those of the Persians!

By fleeing to Memphis, Psammeticus put himself into the position where one more battle would decide the destiny of Egypt. When Cambyses demanded that the capital surrender, his messengers were murdered. Then Cambyses attacked in strength. Firm Egyptian resistance delayed the fall of Memphis for a time, but in the end the city fell to Cambyses, and the land of Egypt entered a new period of history. Psammeticus III was deported to Susa, and Cambyses behaved as a true successor to the Pharaohs. He paid homage to the gods of Egypt and entrusted a high Egyptian official with the administration of the country. Reforms were ordered in the interest of the Egyptian people.

Cambyses determined to become a good Egyptian. As Cyrus had determined to legitimize his claim to the throne of Babylon, so Cambyses determined to ascend the throne of the Pharaohs as a legitimate sovereign. He adopted the royal costume and laid official claim to be the son of the sun-god Re. A firsthand account of Cambyses as he looked in Egyptian eyes was given by Udjahorresne, admiral of the royal fleet under Amasis and Psammeticus, and priest of the goddess Neith at Sais. Udjahorresne was appointed by Cambyses as head physician and served as a companion of the king and major domo of the palace. He prepared the official cartouch which designates Cambyses as "king of Upper and Lower Egypt" and descendant of Re. At the suggestion of Udjahorresne, Cambyses ordered the temple to be cleared of foreigners who had taken residence there.[4] Revenues which had been diverted from the temple at Sais to pay for Greek mercenaries were restored.

3. Herodotus, *Histories* III, 11,12
4. J. Couyat and P. Montet, *Les Inscriptions du Ouadi Hammamat*, No. 164.

Thus religious policy inaugurated by Cyrus seems to have been carried on by Cambyses. In some cases, however, gifts to the temples diminished and the activities of the priests were restricted. Later writers imputed to Cambyses an attitude of cruelty and ruthlessness which does not do justice to his character.

With Egypt firmly under control, Cambyses determined to press on to other African areas and add them to his domains. Carthage was then the dominant power in the western Mediterranean. Carthage had been colonized by Phoenicians, and the Phoenicians of Tyre refused to dispatch their ships against their own flesh and blood. Canaanite influence on the culture of Carthage is mentioned as late as the time of Augustine.

A land expedition of 50,000 men was sent against the Oasis of Ammon, west of Egypt. The expedition passed successfully the oases of el-Khargeh and ed-Dakhlah and continued their march through the desert. The Greek sources which relate this expedition tell us that it was overwhelmed by a sandstorm. The troops were never heard from again. Their utter annihilation is still a mystery. That the efforts of Cambyses to conquer African areas west of Egypt did not end in total failure, however, is evident from the fact that the Greeks of Libya, Cyrene, and Barka submitted.

Greek sources also tell of an expedition into Ethiopia, led personally by Cambyses. Before one-quarter of the distance had been covered, the army ran short of provisions and it was necessary to give orders to retreat. During this campaign Cambyses received news of troubles at home. The throne had been usurped by one who claimed to be his brother Bardiya.

Cambyses remained at Memphis for a short time after his return from the Ethiopian campaign. According to Greek sources, he abandoned his earlier kindly attitude toward Egyptian religion, ridiculed the god Ptah, ordered the statues to be burned, and stabbed to death the Apis-bull at Memphis. Olmstead discounts these tales. He states that the Apis-bull died while Cambyses was on his Ethiopian campaign, and the next Apis-bull, born in the fifth year of Cambyses, survived to the fourth year of Darius.[5]

As the news from Iran became more alarming, Cambyses determined to return home. Egypt was left with garrisons at Daphnae, east of the delta, at Memphis the capital, and at Elephantine at the first cataract of the Nile. The Elephantine

---

5. A. T. Olmstead, *op. cit.*, p. 90 f.

garrison is of particular interest because it was garrisoned by Jewish mercenaries who had a temple of their own and had correspondence with their Palestinian co-religionists (see Chapter VIII).

On the course of his journey homeward, probably in northern Palestine, Cambyses received confirmation of the report of the usurpation of the throne by the pretender Gaumata who had assumed the name of Bardiya, or Smerdes. The new ruler was accepted by nearly all the provinces of the Empire. He attempted to win the favor of the people by remitting taxes for three years, and he attempted a religious reform.

Cambyses never reached home. Herodotus says his death resulted from a wound accidentally self-inflicted when mounting his horse. The Persian record suggests suicide. We know that Cambyses suffered from epileptic fits, and there are evidences of insanity in his latter days, particularly if the reputed atrocities committed in Egypt after his return from the Ethiopian campaign are to be believed.

After Cambyses died, the army remained loyal to the government which he represented. Two months later the pretender Gaumata was taken prisoner and executed. Darius, son of Hystaspes was to become the next Persian monarch.

3

DARIUS, AND THE REORGANIZATION OF THE EMPIRE

Darius claimed to be the legitimate successor of Cambyses. In the eyes of many of his contemporaries he was a usurper. Olmstead entitles his chapter on Darius, "Usurper Darius." The Behistun inscription shows the pains which Darius took to prove that he was the scion of the house of Achemenes. He gives his pedigree thus:

> "My father is Hystaspis; the father of Hystaspis was Arsames; the father of Arsames was Ariyarmenes; the father of Ariyarmenes was Teispes; the father of Teispes was Achaemenes...on that account are we called Achaemenians; from antiquity are we descended; from antiquity hath our race been kings...eight of my race were kings before me, I am the ninth."[1]

Legend states that, after the death of Cambyses, seven Persian nobles, under the leadership of Darius, conspired against the false Bardiya. They agreed to choose as king the one whose horse neighed first after sunrise. Through the ruse of his groom, the throne was won for Darius.

1. Revolt in the Empire

Whatever may be said of Darius' claim to the throne, it was established with the greatest of difficulty. With the assassination of Bardiya, the empire began to split apart. Darius, however, was not one to sit idly by and see the empire dismembered. When but twenty years of age, he had accompanied Cyrus in his campaign against the northwestern mountaineers. He had been in Egypt with Cambyses. Revolts began in Elam and Babylon and spread through most of the empire. Within two years, however, Darius was firmly established as the Persian monarch. To accomplish this, he adopted a policy of firmness reminiscent of the cruelty of Assyrians such as Ashurbanipal. More than once we read of the treatment of a rebel in which

---

1. The Behistun Inscription, col. 1, lines 2-4.

Darius boasts that he "cut off his nose and his ears and his tongue and put out his eyes,"[2] and cast him in fetters at the royal court to be gazed at by the people as a warning that rebellion does not pay.

2. The Behistun Inscription

Darius wanted his victories to be remembered by posterity. He likewise wished to have his contemporaries respect his power. It was the policy of many Pharaohs and kings of the Near East to prepare monuments to commemorate their victories. The stela of the Egyptian Merneptah commemorates a victory in Palestine and is the first Egyptian mention of Israel. The black obelisk of Shalmaneser shows subject peoples, including Jehu of Israel, paying tribute to the Assyrian. The annals of Sennacherib boast of the victories of the Assyrian who besieged Jerusalem and shut up Hezekiah "like a bird in a cage." Cyrus had recorded his choice by Marduk and his benevolent policy toward captive peoples and gods. None of these ever attempted a monument on so grand a scale as the Behistun inscription of Darius. He chose a mountainside on which to record his deeds on imperishable stone. On the main caravan route between Bagdad and Tehran, sixty-five miles from Hamadan, at an altitude of five hundred feet, a series of inscriptions fifty-eight feet, six inches long can still be seen. By the side of the road is a spring where the ancient traveler had to stop. Darius used the techniques of the modern billboard advertiser!

Beneath the symbolic figure of his god, Ahuramazda, stands Darius, with his foot resting on the prostrate form of Gaumata, the false Bardiya. The uplifted hand of Darius demands the attention of the passer-by, insisting that he stop and read. Behind Gaumata are nine men, their hands bound behind their backs and cords about their necks. These are the pretenders and rebels whom Darius has defeated. Behind Darius are two armsbearers.

The inscription itself was written in Old Persian, Babylonian, and Elamite. As a tri-lingual inscription it may be compared with the Egyptian Rosetta Stone. As the Rosetta Stone provided the key to the decipherment of Egyptian hieroglyphics to Champollion and his successors, so the Behistun inscription provided the key to the decipherment of Babylonian (or Akkadian) cuneiform to Rawlinson and later cuneiformists. It would be

---

2. The Behistun Inscription, col. 2, line 13.

hard to exaggerate the value of such studies in helping us to reconstruct the history of the ancient Near East.

3.   Darius and the Jews

The work of rebuilding the Jerusalem Temple, begun as a result of the edict of Cyrus, had come to a halt. The last days of Cyrus and the reign of Cambyses were times of disillusionment and adjustment for the returned exiles. Harassed by unfriendly neighbors, they found they had all they could do to provide for the necessities of this life. The people were agreed on one thing: "The time is not come, the time that the Lord's house should be built" (Hag. 1:2).

This spirit of defeatism was not shared by Haggai and Zechariah, two prophets who began to prophecy to Judah in the second year of Darius. They were aware of the problems which the Jews faced, but theirs was the heroism of faith:

> "Yet now be strong, O Zerubbabel, saith the Lord; and be strong, O Joshua, son of Josedech, the High Priest; and be strong, all ye people of the land, saith the Lord, and work: for I am with you, saith the Lord of hosts: according to the word that I covenanted with you when ye came out of Egypt, so my spirit remaineth among you: fear ye not" (Hag. 2:4-5).

The threats and the promises of Haggai and Zechariah stirred discouraged Judah to renewed activity. The work of rebuilding began in earnest. Perhaps at the instigation of "the adversaries of Judah and Benjamin," the Persian governor "beyond the river," Tattenai (perhaps "Thithinaia" in Persian) made a visit to investigate the activities of the Jews. Anything that savored of rebellion against Darius would be dealt with promptly. Tattenai's question was a pointed one: "Who gave you a decree to build this house and to finish this wall?" (Ezra 5:3). The Jews appealed to the decree of Cyrus, and suggested that a search be made of the royal archives for the royal decree.

In the royal archives at Ecbatana the decree was found. Darius determined that it must be honored. His royal order said: "Let the work of this house of God alone; let the governor of the Jews and the elders of the Jews build this house of God in his place" (Ezra 6:7). He further decreed that funds be given the Jews from the royal treasury to assist in the rebuilding project (Ezra 6:8).

The difficulties of the Jews were not over. The adversaries continued to stir up trouble, but it is to the credit of Darius that he honored the decree of Cyrus and encouraged the Jews in their labors.

In the sixth year of Darius (516 B.C.) the Temple was completed. Special dedicatory sacrifices were offered, and the priests and Levites were assigned their respective tasks (Ezra 6:15-18).

4. Civil Government under Darius

The policy of ruling through native princes, which Cyrus followed, had certain political weaknesses. The opening days of Darius' reign were proof that instability was fostered when the central government was not independently strong. The death of a king was a signal to the native princes to revolt in the hope that the new king would not be able to assert imperial authority.

The institution of the satrapy existed before Darius. The word, in its Persian form *Khshatrapava,* occurs in the Behistun inscription. Darius developed the institution and extended it over all his empire.

In government as organized by Darius, the king was supreme and absolute. Yet there were certain restrictions upon his liberty. The other six of the seven Persian nobles who had conspired against the false Bardiya had extensive land grants. They also had the right to provide the king's wives. Unless the king married within the royal Achemenian line as did Darius, he was permitted to marry only the daughters of the Persian nobles. These men must be consulted on important occasions. Seven counselors might be consulted in matters of lesser importance.[3] On points of law, seven judges, appointed for life, must be consulted. The king was bound by his own decisions, as is reflected in the proverbial expression, "the law of the Medes and Persians which altereth not" (Daniel 6:8, 14, 15; cf. Esther 1:19, 8:8).

Under the king were the satraps, each restricted to his own satrapy. The satrap was a civil governor only. The military chief in the satrapy was independent of the governor, and responsible directly to the king. The chief satrapies were filled by members of the royal house. Where such were not available, the king's daughters might be married to a satrap. Rogers observes, "So complete was the process of appointing in the first instance and of hedging about with surveillance within and without that we hear astonishingly little of malfeasance in office among the satraps."[4]

The disappearance of Zerubbabel from his position as governor of Judah may be a result of the civil reorganization effected

3. Cf. Herodotus, *Histories* VII. 8: Ezra 7:14.
4. Robert William Rogers, *A History of Ancient Persia,* p. 112.

by Darius. There is no hint in the Biblical records that he was removed for sedition, as some have suggested. The fact that his name simply drops out of the Biblical record may suggest that the change of policy which Darius inaugurated resulted in his removal.[5]

The development of roads and the postal system was another of the projects which Darius designed to facilitate the government of his far-flung empire. Several great roads were inherited from the old Assyrian Empire. One of these extended from Babylon to Carchemish, with a connecting spur to Nineveh, and was prolonged westward and southward to Egypt. Another bound Babylon to the heart of Media. Darius rebuilt the road which connected Nineveh to Ecbatana, passing over the Zagros Mountains, and the road from Ecbatana to Sardis passing through Harran with a spur going down to Susa.

The Persian postal system far surpassed all of its predecessors. The network of roads was divided into post routes with horsemen stationed at regular intervals. Any message from king to satrap, or satrap to king, was carried from one stage to the next until it reached its destination. Herodotus' famous description of the Persian Post can be seen engraved across the front of the New York post office: "These neither snow nor rain nor heat nor darkness of night prevent from accomplishing each one his appointed task, with the very utmost speed."[6]

One hundred and eleven post-stations were located along the one thousand six hundred and seventy-seven mile road from Susa to Sardis and Ephesus. The caravans took ninety days to travel this road from end to end. The royal couriers, availing themselves of the fresh relays of horses at the post-stations, covered it in a week.

5. Military Tactics of Darius

The standing army maintained by Darius was surprisingly small. His personal bodyguard consisted of 2,000 cavalry and 2,000 infantrymen of noble birth and 10,000 "immortals" recruited from the Medes and Persians. Further recruits from the Median or Persian nobility might be summoned as needed.

At the most important fortresses, such as Sardis, Memphis, Elephantinae, Daphnae, and Babylon, forces of the standing army were kept. In the event of minor rebellions, the satraps, either alone or in concert with neighboring satraps, were ex-

5. N. H. Snaith, *The Jews from Cyrus to Herod*, p. 17.
6. Herodotus, *Histories* VIII, 98.

pected to find means to restore order. The king himself was responsible for meeting a major threat. The guard was mobilized and a levy was made to secure recruits. Their lack of adequate training would be a weakness in the event of a major attack. The empire suffered only minor skirmishes for a long period, and the military program was adequate for such.

Darius had been most successful in administering his government. Like many another ruler, he could not stand inactivity. Herodotus reports a conversation in which Atossa, Darius' wife, challenged him with the words, "Sire, you are a mighty ruler; why sit you idle, winning neither new dominions nor new power for your Persians?"[7]

In 512 B.C. Darius decided to attack the Scythians. These nomadic people had come southward and westward from the steppes of Russia and had settled north of the Black Sea, and west and south as far as the Danube.

Tales of the Scythians had spread throughout the Persian Empire. They were ready to occupy Thrace, and Asia Minor would be next! Gold mines were abundant in their country, guarded by griffins and worked by harmless ants as large as foxes! The satrap of Cappadocia had crossed the Black Sea and taken several prisoners from among the Scythians. Darius determined to teach the Scythians respect for Persian arms, and add some Scythian gold to the royal treasury at the same time.

Although Darius knew little about the Scythians, he had had dealings with the Greeks, and probably hoped to take the Balkans from the rear, and at the same time, deprive Greece of timber for its fleet. Control of the entire Black Sea region would also cut off much of the wheat supply from Greece.

Greek sources suggest that the army raised by Darius for his Scythian campaign numbered about 700,000. This was the first military encounter between Asia and Europe.

Darius' Greek physician, Democedes, was sent with a fleet to reconnoitre the Greek coast and is thought to have reached Tarentum. A force of thirty more ships explored the western waters of the Black Sea. Byzantium accepted Persian rule. The beginnings of the campaign appeared auspicious.

The army passed over the Straits on a bridge of boats and conquered eastern Thrace with little resistance. They followed the contour of the Black Sea to the mouth of the Danube, then followed the Danube west to the head of the Danube Delta where a bridge was built by the Ionians of Darius' army. It was

7. Herodotus, *Histories* III, 134.

Darius' hope to carry out his land operations in conjunction with the fleet which was to follow along the coast, but the navy and the army soon lost contact and Darius had to plunge into the interior of the country. The Scythians would not stand to give battle, but withdrew before the Persians, forcing the Persians to enter an unknown country. The "scorched earth" policy of the Scythians soon produced real suffering in an army which expected to find its support from the land. Darius was compelled to give up the pursuit of fleeing nomads and retreated toward the Danube bridge and civilization.

The Scythian campaign was not a complete failure. Before recrossing the Bosphorus, a force of 80,000 men was dispatched to complete the conquest of Thrace, and this was successfully carried out. The Persian boundaries were now in contact with the northern Greeks. Macedonia recognized the suzerainty of Darius.

Back in Asia Minor the Greek coastal cities successively fell into the hands of Darius. The centers of the Black Sea wheat trade were all in his hands. Except for Greece itself, Darius was sovereign of the Greek world.

About the time of the Scythian campaign in the west, the Persians decided to descend from the Iranian plateau upon the plain of the Punjab region of India. The project was easily accomplished, and a new satrapy was formed which yielded immense revenues for the Persian crown.

Resisting the temptation to push east to the Ganges, Darius turned his attention to the southeast. He ordered the building of a fleet which was put under the command of Scylax, a Greek admiral in the employ of Darius. For thirty months Scylax explored the Indus River, the Indian Ocean, and the Red Sea.[8]

Darius was interested in exploration because of his desire to connect Egypt with the rest of his empire. Scylax discovered the relation between the Red Sea, the Persian Gulf, and the Indian Ocean.

In the days of Pharaoh Necho an unsuccessful attempt had been made to build a canal between the Nile River and the Gulf of Suez. In 518, while in Egypt, Darius evidently noticed traces of this earlier enterprise. His desire for a cheaper and

8. Aristotle refers to an account of his experiences written by Scylax (*Politics* VII. 14. 2). In modern times it has been questioned by many competent scholars and the episode simply ignored by others. Meyer, *Geschichte des Altertums*, III, p. 99 ff, and Rogers, *op. cit.* p. 119, accept it as true.

more direct route to India caused him to give orders for the
digging of a new canal. Five red-granite stelae were erected along
the banks of the canal. On them Darius declares:

> "I am a Persian. From Parsa I seized Egypt. I commanded this canal
> to be dug from the river, Nile by name, which flows in Egypt, to the
> sea which goes from Parsa. Afterward this canal was dug as I com-
> manded, and ships passed from Egypt through this canal to Parsa as
> was my will."[9]

6. Greek Rebellion

Darius was never able to incorporate the mainland Greeks
into his empire. His successes in Thrace and Macedonia served
to put the democratically minded Greek city states on guard.
Darius tried to interfere in the internal affairs of Athens, which
had a pro-Persian party, but the presence of Persian gold in
Athens had a negative effect. Athens threw in her lot with the
opposition.

The courage of the European Greeks in daring to defy Darius
sparked a revolt of the Ionians who had been Persian subjects.
The Ionian league was re-established, and the aid promised by
European Greece was proclaimed. The Greeks seized Sardis but
had to retreat before Persian reinforcements. Meanwhile the
European Greeks withdrew because of war between Athens and
Aegina. The area suffered at the hands of the Persians to such
an extent that the consequences were felt for two centuries.

Since the revolt of the Ionians had been encouraged by the
European Greeks, Persia decided it must take action against the
continent. A fleet of 600 ships left Asia Minor with the avowed
purpose of strengthening the pro-Persian elements in Greece by
a show of force. Half the ships and about 20,000 men were lost
in a severe storm off Mt. Athos. A second attempt was more successful. Datis, the Median admiral, besieged the Greek city of
Eretria. When it was betrayed into his hands, Datis made the
mistake of burning the temples, destroying the town, and selling
its inhabitants as slaves to Susa. This served to unite the various
factions of Greeks against Persia. They saw clearly that the Persians would show no mercy toward the conquered Greeks.

When Darius landed at Marathon, he was met by the
Athenian army. Before reinforcements could arrive from Sparta,
the Athenians met the Persians and won a resounding victory.
Seven Persian ships were captured by the Greeks, and the re-

9. Diodorus, i. 33.9, claims that the canal was not completed because the
   king was told that the level of the Red Sea was higher than that of
   the Nile, and therefore Egypt would be flooded if the canal were
   actually opened.

mainder withdrew. Troubles in Egypt demanded the attention of Darius, and he gave up his plans for resuming his operations against Greece.

Shortly after Marathon, Egypt was in open revolt against Darius. The heavily garrisoned troops living off the land, and the heavy tribute and taxes demanded by Darius, proved too much for the Egyptians. The Greeks had probably encouraged revolt in Egypt and other trouble spots in the Persian Empire.

7.   The End of Darius

Before the Egyptian revolt was ended, Darius had died. As an organizer of the civil government he has seldom been equaled. The royal palace which he built at Persepolis was one of the great structures of antiquity. Darius could be cruel. He ruled as an absolute monarch. Organizationally, the Persian Empire reached its peak of efficiency under Darius, but decay had already begun to set in.

4

XERXES I, AND THE ATTEMPTED CONQUEST OF GREECE

Xerxes had been carefully groomed as successor to Darius. If some question exists concerning the right of Darius to the throne, the line of Xerxes cannot be challenged. He was the son of Darius by Atossa, a daughter of Cyrus. For twelve years he served under his father as viceroy of Babylon before succeeding to the throne at the death of Darius. The Persian form of the name Xerxes is Khshayarsha, which, in Hebrew, is rendered Ahasuerus (Ezra 4:6 and the Book of Esther).

I. Revolts in the Empire

When, at the age of thirty-five, Xerxes succeeded his father as king, the land of Egypt was in rebellion and the Greek problem had not been resolved. Xerxes acted promptly. Egypt was made submissive to the Persian crown, and Achemenes, a younger brother of Xerxes, was placed in charge.

Babylon next rebelled, with several claimants assuming the royal title "King of Babylon and of the Lands," but Xerxes decided to act. Zopyros was appointed Satrap by Xerxes, only to be slain by the rebellious Babylonians. Megabysos, the son of the slain satrap, was appointed in his stead, and Xerxes determined to thoroughly humble the Babylonians.

The walls of the city were razed by the Persians, and the ornate temples of Babylon were destroyed. The famous temple, Esagila, was demolished, and the golden statue of Bel-Marduk was melted down. Every king who claimed to be the legitimate ruler of Babylon was required to take the hands of this statue of the god of Babylon every New Year's day. In destroying the statue, Xerxes attempted to end the very concept of a continuing Babylonian empire. The title "King of Babylon," which had been part of the royal title of the Persian kings since

Cyrus, was dropped. Xerxes simply called himself "King of Persia and Media," with Babylon continuing as a part of the Persian Empire.

2. Xerxes and Greece

After successfully resolving the problems within the empire, Xerxes turned his attention westward. Careful preparation was made for a simultaneous land and sea attack on Greece, a project attempted but not successfully executed by Darius.

For three years Xerxes planned for the impending invasion. A canal was built to avoid the tempestuous cape of Athos, where Darius had lost a large portion of his fleet. Bridges were erected and provisions were assembled at strategic places in preparation for the attack.

Xerxes recruited his army from forty-six nations. Twenty-nine Persian generals commanded the army, with Xerxes as commander-in-chief. The straits which separate Asia Minor from Europe were spanned by a bridge of boats built by the Phoenicians. Xerxes made a libation to his gods, and cast a cup, a sword, and a bow into the waters to insure success.

Our information comes from the Greek historians, and we suspect that some of their figures are exaggerated. The importance of the invasion, and the subsequent withdrawal of Xerxes, can hardly be exaggerated, however.

The fleet of Xerxes numbered, we are told, 1,207 fighting vessels with additional large ships driven by as many as fifty oars. The number of transports — 3,000 — is almost certainly an exaggeration. The ships were manned by the Phoenicians, but among the navigators were also Cypriots, Ionians, Cilicians, and Hellespontese. Four hundred and seven Greek ships are said to have been enlisted in Xerxes' navy.

After spending the winter in Sardis, the armies of Xerxes crossed the bridge from Asia to Europe in May or June, 480 B.C. The fleet then sailed to Sarpedon. In the meantime Xerxes sent heralds to the Greek cities to give them an opportunity to submit voluntarily. They were asked to send back earth and water in token of their submission.

While Xerxes was temporarily encamped at Therma, the heralds made their reports. A few brought earth and water, but most of Greece was determined to fight for its independence. Early in August, Xerxes began to move forward.

Athens and Sparta resolved their own differences and formed a coalition to fight the Persians. They appealed to all the Greeks to join them in fighting for their liberty. They met with considerable, but not universal, success. Argos and Crete adopted a policy of neutrality.

The early battles were disastrous for the Greeks. Thessaly was lost in spite of the valiant fighting of ten thousand heavily armed infantry who had been sent to guard the vale of Tempe. The middle of Greece was next under attack and the Greeks determined to hold Mt. Oeta, which was flanked on the right by the Euboean Straits and the Gulf of Malis. Ten thousand men under the Spartan, Leonidas, determined to defend the only road through the pass at Thermopylae. A Greek fleet was sent to meet the Persian navy at Artemisium.

A storm destroyed three of the Greek ships sent to Artemisium, but the Persians lost, according to Greek figures, four hundred ships of war, and a larger number of transports off the Artemisium promontory. Fifteen Persian ships seeking refuge from the storm were captured by the Greeks.

The Spartans, under Leonidas, were prepared to check the advance of the Persians into central Greece, but Greece was betrayed by a Malian named Ephialtes. The Persians were shown a path over the mountain to the rear of the Greeks. The Spartans fought to the end, and Leonidas became a hero by dying at his post. The Persians, however, won an important objective, for mid-Greece had opened before them. By August Xerxes was in Athens. He burned the temples on the acropolis, allegedly in revenge for the burning of Sardis.

The goals of Xerxes appeared about to be realized. Xerxes hoped to complete the conquest of Greece by engaging the Greek fleet which was concentrated at Salamis. The Greeks had about 380 ships, only half the number the Persians could place in battle. Yet the Battle of Salamis, September 27th or 28th, 480 B.C., became one of the decisive battles of history. The destruction of Athens had shown the Greeks that their culture and civilization would not be respected by a conqueror like Xerxes. Fighting for their homes and their lives, the Greeks so thoroughly defeated the Persians at Salamis that the Persian fleet, with Xerxes, was forced to flee.

The Persians still had a large land army, and Xerxes entrusted the Greek campaign to Mardonius, one of his generals. First seeking success through diplomacy, Mardonius was unable to make any headway with the Greeks.

Mardonius next fought a series of battles designed to bring Greece finally to her knees before Persia. Much of Attica was despoiled and Mardonius moved on to Boeotia. The Greeks of the Peloponnesus took the offensive, however. Mardonius was defeated at Meggara. A defensive position was taken by Mardonius between Plataea and the river Asopus. With 50,000 Asiatic troops and 10,000 Greek allies he awaited attack. Twelve thousand Spartans, heavily armed, joined other Greeks to make a comparable army of 50,000 poised against the Persians. In cavalry, Mardonius had an advantage, but otherwise the armies were of comparable strength.

After ten days of waiting for favorable omens, Mardonius used his cavalry to attack the Greeks. The Persians were decisively defeated. The Greeks, who had been warned of the impending attack, were able to make the best use of their forces. Mardonius was slain and his army fled, leaving immense stores of provisions and booty in the field. Herodotus says that not 3,000 Persians remained alive, although this is considered to be an exaggeration.

At the same time the Athenians succeeded in conquering Persia's Greek allies. Before autumn the entire Hellespont area was in Greek hands. The following spring Byzantium, the last Persian stronghold in the Greek world, fell, and the bitter struggle between the Persians and the Greeks was ended.

3.   The Close of Xerxes' Reign

After the Greek debacle, Xerxes was not to distinguish himself again on the field of battle. He lived fourteen years after the loss of Greece, but little is known about them. He was murdered by a usurper, Artabanus, who is said to have reigned seven months before being killed by Artaxerxes, the third son and legitimate heir of Xerxes. The first son born after the king's accession to the throne was regarded as legitimate successor.

4.   Xerxes and the Bible

There is only one brief reference to Xerxes in the annals of Palestinian Judaism. Ezra 4:6 is the one Biblical reference which bridges the fifty-eight year period between the dedication of the Temple and the arrival of Ezra in the seventh year of Artaxerxes. The only information we have states that "the people of the land," that is, the Samaritans, Edomites, and other enemies of Judah, in the beginning of the reign of Ahasuerus (Xerxes) wrote an accusation against the inhabitants of Judah and Jerusalem.

Xerxes seems to have been too busy elsewhere to trouble himself with the problems of Judah. The period was one of frustration and disappointment for the Jews who were looking for deliverance from their foes.

The lot of the Jews who had chosen not to return to Judah is described in the Book of Esther. The virtuous Vashti was deposed by Xerxes who searched the realm for a suitable substitute. Esther, who was not known to be a Jewess, was chosen as the fairest maiden in the empire and brought to be a wife to Xerxes. When the royal favorite, Haman, determined to rid himself of the hated Mordecai, cousin and guardian of Esther, along with all the Jews of the realm, Mordecai urged Esther to intercede with Xerxes on behalf of her people. He was convinced that she had "come to the kingdom for such a time as this." She risked her life by seeking an audience with the king. Xerxes received her kindly, however. He determined to save the Jews from the persecution that had been decreed. Haman was hanged on the gallows which he had prepared for Mordecai. The Jewish feast of Purim commemorates this deliverance of the Jews in the days of Esther.

Xerxes was reputed to act habitually like a spoilt child. The Esther episode agrees well with this description. He was given to ostentation and loved display, and appears to have been susceptible to the flattery and intrigue of fawning courtiers. Religiously he was a Zoroastrian, which may account, in part, for his willingness to destroy the Bel-Marduk temple in Babylon. He was assassinated by the captain of his bodyguard, Artabanus, in the twentieth year of his reign.

5

ARTAXERXES I, AND THE LOSS OF PERSIAN PRESTIGE

The age of Artaxerxes is one of the best documented periods of classical antiquities. Herodotus, the "father of history," was traveling throughout the world and writing his famous histories. Pericles was in power in Athens. The famous monuments of the Parthenon were built during the Periclean age, and Athens reached the zenith of its culture and influence.

Artaxerxes Longimanus (i.e., "the long handed" because his right hand was reputedly longer than his left hand) had the usual problem of putting down rebellions in various parts of the realm when he became king of the Persian Empire. The efficient governmental system of Darius had been weakened during the reign of Xerxes, with the result that rebellion was more likely to succeed. Hystaspes, a brother of Artaxerxes, attempted to assert independent rule in Bactria, but Artaxerxes acted quickly and forcefully to re-establish his own royal authority.

Disturbances in Egypt gave Artaxerxes more cause for concern. Familiar with Greek defiance of Persia, many in Egypt hoped for a similar position of independence. Inaros, a son of the Pharaoh Psammeticus, was recognized as king by a group of the nomes of the eastern Delta. Achemenes, son of Darius and brother of Xerxes, represented the Persian interests in Egypt. While Artaxerxes was putting down the Bactrian revolt, Achemenes appeared in Persia to seek help in bringing Egypt into submission. An army was raised, and Achemenes returned to Egypt.

Achemenes defeated Inaros in the initial battle. A Greek fleet of two hundred vessels subsequently came to the aid of the rebellious Egyptians, and most of the city of Memphis was lost to the Persians. Artaxerxes raised a new army under the leadership of Megabyzos and enlisted the aid of a Phoenician navy under Artabazos. A decisive battle was fought in the Delta, and Inaros was wounded. The Egyptians and their Greek allies barricaded themselves in Prosopitis for eighteen months. Unable to dislodge them by military attack, the Persians diverted the branch of the Nile in which the Greek fleet was anchored. The desperate crew burned the ships before surrendering to the Persians. The Phoenicians sank a fleet of fifty Greek triremes which had been sent to reinforce the rebels. Thus the rebellion in Egypt was put down, but Persia had had to pay a large price to retain control over Egypt.

At this time Ezra "the scribe" requested permission of Artaxerxes to lead a fresh group of Jews back to Judea. Ezra was called "the scribe of the law of the God of heaven." Olmstead suggests that this would be equivalent to "Secretary of State for Jewish Affairs." Ezra would thus be responsible to the king for the Jewish community.

Jews had prospered in Babylonia during the Persian rule. Great business houses like that of the Murashu family of Nippur have left us cuneiform texts which describe the details of their extensive business enterprise.[1] While the more worldly minded would have little concern for the settlement which had been established in Jerusalem in the days of Cyrus, the spiritually minded knew that God was working out His purposes through that remnant that had returned.

Ezra gathered together 1,500 such Babylonian Jews as a group of colonists who would reinforce and assist the earlier settlers, and help accomplish the necessary rebuilding and defense operations. In the seventh year of Artaxerxes I the group organized at Ahava, a district in Babylonia. Bearing gold, silver, and Temple utensils, they started out on a journey which would take them over five months to complete.

Arriving safely on the twelfth day of the seventh month, Ezra lost no time in beginning his ministry. The reading and interpretation of the Law, and its enforcement, particularly in the matter of mixed marriages, occupied much of his time and energies. It should be remembered that he was acting on the authority of the Persian government, and that his decrees were binding in a political as well as in a religious sense.

Men who had returned from Babylon were frequently guilty of divorcing their lawful Jewish wives and marrying the women

---

1. H. V. Hilprecht and A. T. Clay, *Business Documents of Murashu Sons of Nippur.*

of the land. In pre-exilic days mixed marriages had been a temptation. Solomon was led astray by his foreign wives. The restored community must, according to Ezra's interpretation of Scripture, rid itself of the "daughters of the peoples of the lands." The people were ordered to assemble in Jerusalem, under penalty of the "devotion" (i.e., destruction) of their property and exclusion from the congregation. At the appointed assembly the divorce of alien wives was accepted in principle, with provision for detailed examination of individual cases.

Enemies of Judah sought to find some excuse to prevent the Jews from fortifying and protecting the city of Jerusalem. Ever since the first return the adversaries had been at work. In the days of Artaxerxes a letter of accusation was addressed to the Persian king in which the Jews were accused of plotting rebellion against the crown. Artaxerxes, nervous at the thought of rebellion, ordered the Jews to stop their rebuilding operations until he should make a further decree (Ezra 4:1-21). The enemies of Judah used force (Ezra 4:23) to prevent the Jews from completing their work of rebuilding the city walls. It is this state of affairs that challenged Nehemiah.

In the court of Artaxerxes in Susa (or Shushan), Nehemiah was functioning as royal cupbearer. The exact nature of his work is not known, but his was a position of importance which brought him into close terms with the king. When the king learned of the distress of heart which plagued Nehemiah, he gave him a leave of absence to return to Jerusalem to assist in repairing the broken walls.

With an armed escort, Nehemiah reached Jerusalem and surveyed the needs of the city. He summoned the leaders of the city and assured them that God's hand was upon him. Unitedly they began to build. The old enemies of the Jews were as active as ever. A cry of rebellion was made. They attempted to lure Nehemiah to a conference in the valley of Ono. They charged Nehemiah with assuming royalty. Nehemiah disregarded the charges of the enemy and patiently continued his work.

In spite of opposition from without and from within, the walls went up, the gates were set in place, and the city was able to function once more. A city without walls was no city at all, according to ancient standards.

The completion of the work was enthusiastically celebrated. Ezra and Nehemiah headed processions which moved around the walls in opposite directions, meeting near the site of the

Temple. Sacrifices were offered, and the sound of rejoicing was heard afar off.

With pomp and ceremony the populace gathered in the Temple courts to hear the reading of God's Word and to pledge their obedience to its precepts. It was probably the Pentateuch that Ezra had in his hands as he read the Law of the Lord. The Feast of Tabernacles was observed as the people rejoiced in the goodness of God.

After an absence of twelve years, Nehemiah returned to Susa to report to the king. He had no sooner left Jerusalem than the old problems began to reappear. The enemies came back on the scene to make trouble, the Levites did not receive the dues to which they were entitled, the laws of the sabbath were forgotten, and foreign marriages became common again. The children were heard speaking the languages of their non-Jewish mothers (Neh. 13:23, 24).

Nehemiah made a second trip to Jerusalem. Dependent on God to help him enforce the divine Law, Nehemiah accomplished a second reformation of the religious and civil life of Jerusalem. With this, both the Book of Nehemiah and the history of the Old Testament comes to a close.

Artaxerxes was not in the position to strengthen his holdings in the west, and the decline of the Persian Empire is usually dated from his reign. Egypt and Cyprus were still subject to Persia, but most of the rest of the west was gone. The Athenian fleet dominated the eastern Mediterranean. Thrace was self-governing. The conquests of Cyrus in Ionia were in Greek hands.

6

THE LATTER ACHEMENIANS, APPROACHING THE END

The reign of Darius II was one of intrigue and corruption. Although no battles were fought with the Greeks, Persian gold was used to incite Athens against Sparta in the Peloponnesian War. Persian influence over the Greek cities of Asia Minor was thus strengthened.

Minor successes did not change the pattern of history, however. Revolts continued throughout the Persian Empire. The Medes rebelled. Egypt was restive. The Jewish temple at Elephantine was destroyed, but Persia was unable to punish the insurgents.

Artaxerxes II barely missed being killed by his brother Cyrus during his coronation ceremony at Persepolis. At the intreaty of his mother, Artaxerxes pardoned Cyrus. Returning to his satrapy, Cyrus again plotted rebellion. He raised an army and came close to winning a decisive battle near Babylon. Cyrus was a man of courage. He might have arrested the decline of the dynasty had he occupied the throne. But he was killed in battle, and the dreams of his followers were dissipated.

The story of the Greek contingent in Cyrus' army was immortalized by Xenophon. After the disastrous battle of Cunaxa (401 B.C.), the Ten Thousand, as the Greeks were called, fought their way back home, passing through hostile territory and harried by the Persians under Tissaphernes. After the Greek generals had been killed by the Persians, Xenophon was chosen as one of the leaders of the retreat. He led the Ten Thousand up the Tigris, past the ruins of Nineveh (now a forgotten city), to the Black Sea and Byzantium. Xenophon's account of this famous retreat in *The Anabasis* became one of the great books of military science in the ancient world.

Although Persian arms were weak, Artaxerxes was able to

maintain some prestige at home and abroad by the use of Persian gold. In Greece, Athens and Sparta were played off against one another to the benefit of Persia. The Greek cities of Asia Minor were subject to Artaxerxes, and opposition found a quick response. Persian forces on land and sea maintained control over the Ionian Greeks, although the glory of Persia was a thing of the past.

Within Persia new problems arose. A number of the satrapies had become powerful, hereditary offices. High taxes were imposed on the native population, with the result that revolt was fomented. Egypt had declared its independence at the accession of Artaxerxes and had never been reconquered. Cyprus, Phoenicia, and Syria took advantage of Persian weakness to follow suit. Revolts of peasants and artisans were savagely repressed, but the disintegration of the empire continued. One after another the western satrapies all fell away from the empire. They formed a coalition and issued their own coinage.

When Egypt, allied with Sparta and the rebel satraps, marched against Artaxerxes, the empire seemed doomed. A reprieve came, however, when a revolt against Pharaoh Takhos made it necessary for Egypt to abandon its plans and surrender. The threat against Persia was relieved for the time being, but disturbances continued until the death of Artaxerxes II.

Before its downfall, the Achemenian Persian Empire was to enjoy one more period of power. Artaxerxes III determined to rule with the strength of a Darius the Great. He began his reign by murdering all his brothers and sisters — several dozen in all. Sidon, which had sympathized with rebellious Egypt, was burnt and left in ruins. Egypt was reconquered, its cities taken, and their walls razed. Persia was again in a position to menace the Greeks.

Hellenism existed as a cultural if not a political force. Patriotic Greeks urged all who shared Greek culture to unite against the Persians. The mainland Greeks lacked the unity which could accomplish such a mission. To the north, however, Macedon was ruled by an energetic leader who became the dominant personality among the Greeks.

Prodded by the oratory of Demosthenes, Athens concluded an alliance with Persia. Philip of Macedon interpreted this as an unfriendly gesture. In 338 B.C. Philip and his son Alexander won a decisive victory over Athens. The Persian threat was removed, but Greek independence was also destroyed. Philip of Macedon and his son Alexander (later "the Great") now held the destiny of Greece. In the same year Artaxerxes was poisoned.

The murderer of Artaxerxes was Bagoas, a eunuch who had political ambitions of his own. Bagoas spared the life of Arses, the youngest son of Artaxerxes, expecting to use him as a puppet ruler. When Arses showed evidence of having a mind of his own, Bagoas poisoned him also.

In looking for someone whom he might trust, Bagoas chose a cousin of Artaxerxes III who had distinguished himself in battle and had become satrap of Armenia. Bagoas had chosen unwisely again, however. The new monarch took the name of Darius III. Fearing the power and treachery of Bagoas, Darius had him poisoned.

Darius III became king of Persia in 336 B.C. The same year twenty-year-old Alexander ascended the throne in faraway Macedonia with a commission from his father to make war upon Persia. The tide of empire moved toward Alexander and away from Darius. In 333 B.C. Darius was defeated in the battle of Issus. Two years later the center of the empire was pierced by Alexander's victory at Gaugemela, or Arbela. Darius fled to Ecbatana, and then on to Bactria, where he was murdered by his cousin Bessus who took command of the unsuccessful opposition to Alexandria in Bactria.

It is probable that Darius III is the "Darius the Persian" mentioned in Nehemiah 12:22. According to Josephus[1], Jaddua, who is listed as a contemporary of "Darius the Persian," was also a contemporary of Alexander the Great.

With the death of Darius III the empire founded by Cyrus the Great came to an end. The dynasty is named after Achemenes, a minor ruler of a mountainous district in southwestern Iran. The period of ancient Persia's greatness extended from about 550 B.C. to 330 B.C.

---

1. *Antiquities* xi. 8. 4.

7

THE PROBLEMS AND PROGRESS OF THE JEWS

I. The Samaritans

The name Samaria first appears in the Bible as the name of the capital of the northern kingdom. Omri and Ahab built luxurious palaces there, and on occasion the name of the capital is used for the whole kingdom. Samaria was the last city of Israel to fall to the Assyrians. In 722/721 a large number of influential citizens were deported to various cities of the Assyrian Empire. Conversely, colonies of non-Jews from Babylonia, Syria, and Elam were settled in Samaria (II Kings 17:24-29). The result was a mixed population and a disposition to worship Yahweh as the god of the land, along with a reverence for the other gods which the new settlers had formerly worshiped.

The latter kings of Judah, particularly Hezekiah (during whose reign Samaria fell) and Josiah seem to have attempted to expand their borders northward to include some of the territory formerly ruled from Samaria. Faithful Yahwists made their way down to the Jerusalem Temple and relations between Samaria and Judah were quite cordial.

The destruction of Jerusalem and the Babylonian exile, taking place about a century and a half after the fall of Samaria, seem to have changed the picture somewhat. During the time that there was no effective government in Jerusalem, the Samaritans and other neighbors of the Jews were able to occupy former Judean territory and develop a new economy in which the Jews-in-exile had no part. Such Jews as remained in Palestine doubtless made their peace with their neighbors, and a new mode of life was developed.

When the first settlers returned to Jerusalem, following the decree of Cyrus (536 B.C.), the Samaritans and their neighbors faced a crisis. If the Jews were to become independently strong, the possessions of the Samaritans might be threatened. From the earliest days of their settlement, the returned exiles met with difficulty from the Samaritans and their other neighbors.

The Samaritans offered to help in the rebuilding operations, but they were rebuffed. The Jews had learned that co-operation with the idolater would bring the judgment of God. They chose to labor on alone.

When Sanballat, the governor of Samaria under the Persians, was unable to get at the Jewish problem by co-operation, he chose the path of attempted coercion. Neither threats nor armed intervention succeeded, however. The Jews were able to rebuild Temple and walls without outside help and in spite of outside interference.

One of the burdens of Ezra and Nehemiah was that of the mixed marriages of many of the colonists who had returned from Babylon. One of the sons of Joiada, the High Priest, married a daughter of Sanballat, governor of Samaria. This was not only a mixed marriage, but a marriage with an avowed enemy. When the son of the priest, Manasseh by name, refused to give up his Samaritan bride, Nehemiah expelled him.

We know that the Samaritans had a temple on Mt. Gerizim which was destroyed by the Jews in the days of John Hyrcanus. Josephus says that this temple was built by Sanballat for Manasseh so that he could both function as priest and be married to Sanballat's daughter. Other priests who refused to divorce their non-Jewish brides are said to have joined Manasseh (*Antiquities* XI. vii, viii). The Josephus account is repudiated by some scholars, including Montgomery, who regards it simply as a midrash on Nehemiah.

In succeeding years the Jews and the Samaritans became bitter enemies. The statement in John 4, "The Jews have no dealings with the Samaritans," had behind it years of bitterness between the two peoples. It is noteworthy that Jesus saw fit to go through Samaria and thus show that His disciples were not to allow any restrictions to be placed on the preaching of the gospel. The Parable of the Good Samaritan and the miracle in which the Samaritan is commended as the one who returned to thank God for cleansing from leprosy further illustrate the attitude which Jesus commended toward those who would be looked upon as aliens from the commonwealth of Israel.

2. The Jews of Elephantine

During the years 1907 and 1908 excavations were carried on

at the island of Elephantine, ancient Yeb, opposite Assuan (Syene, Ezekiel 29:10; 30:6) at the first cataract of the Nile. Many ancient papyri written in Aramaic were discovered. They were written by Jews between the years 494 and 400 B.C. Most of them were business documents, involving contracts for loans, conveyance of property, and similar activities. The names used are familiar to all readers of the Bible. They include Hosea, Azariah, Zephaniah, Jonathan, Zechariah, Nathan, and Azariah.

The most interesting document is a letter written in 407 B.C. and addressed to Bigvai, the governor of Judea. It tells how Egyptian priests, with the connivance of the local governor and the active assistance of the governor's son, destroyed the temple which the Jews had built at Elephantine:

> "They entered that temple and razed it to the ground. The stone pillars that were there they smashed. Five 'great' gateways built with hewn blocks of stone which were in that temple, they demolished ... and their roof of cedar wood, all of it ... and whatever else was there, everything they burnt with fire. As for the basins of gold and silver and other articles that were in that temple, they carried all of them off and made them their own."[1]

The Egyptian priests resented the sanctuary of an alien deity in their midst, and determined to cleanse their land of its defilement. They doubtless found enough anti-Jewish sentiment among the people to implement their purposes.

The Elephantine Jews asked help in rebuilding their temple.[2]

> "Now your servants Yedoniah and his colleagues and the Jews, the citizens of Elephantine, all say thus: If it please our lord, take thought of this temple to rebuild it, since they do not let us rebuild it. Look to your well-wishers and friends here in Egypt. Let a letter be sent from you to them concerning the temple of the God Yaho, to build it in the fortress of Elephantine as it was built before; and the meal-offering, incense, and burnt offering will be offered in your name and we shall pray for you at all times, we, and our wives, and our children, and the Jews who are here, all of them if you do thus, so that that temple is rebuilt. And you shall have a merit before Yaho the God of Heaven more than a man who offers to him burnt offering and sacrifices worth a thousand talents of silver and (because of) gold. Because of this we have written to inform you. We have also set the whole matter forth in a letter in our name to Delaiah and Shelemiah, the sons of Sanballat the governor of Samaria. Also, Arsames[3] knew nothing of all that was done to us. On the twentieth of Marheshwan, year 17 of King Darius."[4]

The Elephantine Jews, while much concerned about the temple and worship of the God of Israel, whom they called Yahu or Yaho, did not maintain the purity of worship insisted

1. Pap. 1. 9-13; H. L. Ginsberg's Translation.
2. Pap. 1, 22-30, op. cit.
3. Arsames was the satrap of Egypt. According to an earlier passage in the papyrus (4,5) he was in the Persian court during the time of the outrage.
4. Darius II, 424-405 B.C.

on by the prophets of Israel. Among the other gods whom they worshiped were Ishumbethel, Herembethel, 'Anathbethel and 'Anathyahu. Anath was the Canaanite goddess of fertility and war, sister and consort of Baal. The name at Elephantine seems to imply that she was there regarded as the consort of Yahu.

The very existence of a temple and fully developed sacrificial system indicates that the Elephantine Jews rejected the concept of a single central sanctuary as the place to which sacrifices to Yahu (Yahweh) must be brought. Through much of the history of the divided kingdom a conflict existed between those who advocated a central sanctuary and those who preferred the multitudinous "high places." The unity of the God of Israel was inherent in the concept of a central sanctuary, and reformers like Josiah (621 B.C.) insisted on destroying the "high places" as centers of idolatry. The pagan elements in the religion of the Elephantine Jews would underscore the necessity for insisting on the Jerusalem Temple as the one place where sacrifice might be offered.

The Elephantine Jews doubtless considered themselves to be wholly orthodox. Their letters mention the observance of the Jewish Passover and the Feast of Unleavened Bread. A priesthood and sacrificial system patterned after that of the Jerusalem Temple functioned at Elephantine. The fact that appeals are made to Samaria as well as to Jerusalem indicates that the Elephantine Jews did not deem it necessary to take sides in the conflicts between Jerusalem and Samaria.

The origin of the Elephantine community has puzzled scholars, and no theory that has been propounded is without its problems. Contacts, favorable and unfavorable, had been maintained between Israelites and Egypt from Patriarchal times. When Jeroboam found it necessary to flee from King Solomon, he found sanctuary in Egypt. A party friendly to Egypt had existed in both Samaria and Jerusalem before the destruction of these capital cities by the Assyrians and Babylonians. Jeremiah had urged Zedekiah not to heed the pro-Egyptian party, but the promise of aid from Egypt was a deciding factor in Zedekiah's defiance of Nebuchadnezzar. Jeremiah was taken to Egypt where he presumably spent his last days.

One of the Elephantine papyri clearly indicates that the Jewish colony there antedates the invasion of Egypt by Cambyses, the son and successor of Cyrus: "Now our forefathers built this temple in the fortress of Elephantine back in the days of the Kingdom of Egypt, and when Cambyses came to Egypt he found it built. They knocked down all the temples of the gods of Egypt, but no one did any damage to this temple."[5]

The apocryphal *Letter of Aristeas* states that Jews entered Egypt with "the Persian" (Cambyses), and that others had earlier come to Egypt to fight as mercenaries in the army of Pharaoh Psammeticus. Herodotus tells us that Psammeticus II (593-588 B.C.) waged war with the Ethiopians. This leads to the supposition that the Jewish mercenaries were used by Psammeticus in this war, after which they were garrisoned at Elephantine, near the Egyptian-Ethiopian border.

If this reconstruction of the history is correct, the settlement which produced the Elephantine papyri was comprised of the descendants of these earlier settlers, possibly augmented by fresh recruits from Palestine, all of whom were now serving in the Persian army.

While this view appears plausible, and cannot be ruled out as a possibility, there are several problems. The language of the papyri is Aramaic, rather than Hebrew. It would be supposed that Jews coming to Egypt before the exile would have brought their mother tongue with them. A further problem is one of chronology. Psammeticus II was on the throne of Egypt during the years immediately preceding the fall of Jerusalem to Nebuchadnezzar. Are we to picture Jewish soldiers forsaking their own land to fight in the army of Psammeticus against the Ethiopians? Psammeticus seems to have had access to Greek mercenaries, so that there would have been no real need for Jewish recruits.

Another theory, suggested by W. O. E. Oesterley, maintains that the Elephantine Colony was comprised of northern Israelites from Assyria. It is suggested that the second generation of the captives who were removed from Israel after the fall of Samaria were enrolled, either voluntarily or by compulsion, in the army of Ashurbanipal. After Ashurbanipal's conquest of Egypt, Assyrian garrisons were stationed in various parts of the country. The Assyrian hold on Egypt was short-lived, however. Ashurbanipal's victories dated from 667 B.C., but by 663 B.C. Psammeticus I had cleared out the Assyrian garrisons. Oesterley assumes that Psammeticus recognized the Elephantine garrison as Israelite, and permitted the Israelites to enlist in his own army. He suggests that these Israelites would be glad to remain away from Assyria. The language of that part of the Assyrian Empire from which they came was Aramaic, hence the Aramaic of the Elephantine papyri.

---

5 Pap. 1, 14-15, *op. cit.*

Oesterley's view also helps explain the reason for addressing a request for aid to the Samaritans. Presumably the larger part of the community owed its ancestral origins to Samaria. The elements of paganism at Elephantine have something in common with the Scriptural description of the Samaritans who "feared Yahweh" but also served other gods.

While a final word concerning the origin of the Elephantine community cannot yet be given, and no view is without objections, the existence of the community shows us something of the development of Jewish religion during the Persian period. If a reformer like Nehemiah appears Puritanical in his attitude toward his Samaritan neighbors, Elephantine shows the danger which beset a community which left its moorings and allowed a religious syncretism in which Yahweh could be associated with a pantheon of deities.

3. The Synagogue
Origin of the Synagogue

During the time between the Old Testament and the New Testament period, there arose the institution which was to become the focal point of Jewish life through the centuries. No record has been left of the origin of synagogue worship. Jewish tradition suggests that the first synagogues were established during the time of Babylonian exile.

Pre-exilic Judaism looked to the Jerusalem Temple as the focal point of its spiritual life. Worship at local shrines, or "high places," continued through much of Israelite history, but the prophets, and the kings who supported them, abolished such worship and insisted on the primacy of the Temple. In this way the unity of the God of Israel was emphasized, in contrast to the concept of local gods which was prevalent in the ancient world. Jeremiah complained of his generation, ". . . according to the number of thy cities are thy gods, O Judah" (2:28).

When the armies of Nebuchadnezzar destroyed Jerusalem with its Temple, a new orientation was demanded in the worship of the Israelite. According to popular views, a god was expected to protect his people, and the victory of an enemy meant that the gods of the enemy were the strongest of the contending divine beings. Wars were fought on two levels — human and divine. The strongest god would win.

Many in Israel doubtless shared these viewpoints, for the temptation to idolatry and conformity with the current religious practices and ideals was an ever present one. This was not true, however, of those religious leaders of the Jews whom we call the prophets. Defeat in battle did not mean that the God of Israel was weaker than the gods of the Babylonians. It meant that Israel's God was chastening His rebelling people. The prophets saw a divine purpose in Israel's calamities. Daniel writes, "The Lord gave Jehoiakim king of Judah into his (Nebuchadnezzar's) hand" (1:2). The destruction of the Temple was not an evidence of the weakness of Israel's God, but an evidence of His holiness.

Psalm 137 describes the attitude of exiles in Babylon. They are in a strange land, weeping at the remembrance of Zion. Their captors ask them to sing one of the songs of Zion, but Israel protests, "How shall we sing the Lord's song in a strange land?" They remember Jerusalem, and long for the day of restoration.

All evidence, including the prophetic word of Jeremiah, indicated that the exile would be a long one. Before Jerusalem fell, Jeremiah had written to the exiles who had been deported earlier, "Build ye houses, and dwell in them; and plant gardens and eat the fruit of them; take ye wives and beget sons and daughters; and take wives for your sons, and give your daughters to husbands . . . and seek the peace of the city whither I have caused you to be carried away captives, and pray unto the Lord for it, for in the peace thereof shall ye have peace" (29:5-7).

With the destruction of the Temple, sacrifices ceased. Prayer, and the study of the sacred Scriptures, however, knew no geographical limitations. The Book of Ezekiel describes the elders of Israel gathering in the prophet's house (8:1; 20:1-3). Such gatherings became more regular and more organized in nature, resulting in the weekly synagogue services, after which the weekly services in the Christian church were patterned.

The word "synagogue" is of Greek origin, meaning a gathering of people, or a congregation. The Hebrew word for such a gathering is *keneseth,* the name used for the parliament in the modern state of Israel. The word *synagogue* is used for the local congregation of Jews and also for the building in which the community meets for its assemblies and services. In Hebrew the building may be referred to as the *beth hakkeneseth,* "the house of assembly."

With the return from exile following the decree of Cyrus, a second Temple was built in Jerusalem. This again became the focal point of Jewish religious life until its destruction in A.D. 70. Large numbers of Jews did not return to Palestine, however, and the institution of the synagogue continued to fill the spiritual needs of Jews who remained in "the dispersion," whether in Babylon, other cities of the Persian Empire, Egypt, or — later — the cities of Asia Minor, Greece, and Rome. In New Testament times we read: "For from early generations Moses has had in every city those who preach him, for he is read every sabbath in the synagogues" (Acts 15:21).

For the Jews who returned to Palestine, the synagogue became the place of prayer and Bible study, as the Temple served as the place of sacrifice and the center of the great annual convocations. In Nehemiah 8 we read of a great gathering for the public reading of the "Book of the Law of Moses." Ezra made use of a pulpit, or platform, from which he read and explained the Scriptures to the assembled throngs. The fact that the Scriptures were written in Hebrew, and that Aramaic was the spoken language of post-exilic Judaism, provided a further reason for gatherings to translate and interpret the ancient Scripture. In Palestine, as in the dispersion, a quorum of ten heads of families could organize a synagogue.

In the larger towns a body of twenty-three elders formed the sanhedrin, or governing body of the synagogue community. In smaller communities the number of elders was seven. These elders *(presbuteroi)* are sometimes called rulers, *(archontes)*. From this group one was designated "chief ruler" *(gerousiarches)*. The sanhedrin served as a court, and in Judea it represented the civil as well as the religious government. Punishment of scourging, excommunication, and death could be decreed. Scourging was inflicted in the synagogue building. It consisted of "forty stripes save one" (cf II Cor. 11:24; Josephus *Antiquities* iv. 8:21). Excommunication was regarded as a more serious sentence. In its earliest form it meant absolute and final exclusion from the Jewish community. The Hebrew term descriptive of this is *herem*. This is the equivalent of the Greek *anathema*, descriptive of one who is under the curse of God. A temporary excommunication (Hebrew *nidduy*) later developed as a severe rebuke to those whose transgression was not so outrageous as to evoke the *anathema*.

Although the sanhedrin could impose the death penalty in extreme cases, under the Roman rule capital punishment required the confirmation of the Roman procurator (cf. John 18:31).

Each community had its local sanhedrin, but that of Jerusalem attained the eminence of the highest Jewish judicatory. This became known as the Great Sanhedrin. It was presided over by the High Priest and met in a hall associated with the Temple structure. Scribes and the most eminent members of the high-priestly families were associated with the Great Sanhedrin. Its mandates were recognized wherever Jews dwelt (cf. Acts 9:2).

Synagogue Worship

The worship services of the synagogue enjoyed great freedom. Any competent Israelite could officiate. The liberty which was accorded the apostle Paul illustrates this fact.

The leaders of the worship at the synagogue were not the same as those who cared for the legal side of the life of the community, although the same persons could serve in both capacities. The "ruler of the synagogue" (archisunagogos) supervised the service and assumed responsibility for the care and order of the synagogue building. The hazzan, or "minister" (A.V.), of the synagogue brought the Scriptures to the reader and replaced them in their receptacle after the lesson had been read. He served as the agent of the sanhedrin in scourging offenders, and is thought by some to have been responsible for the teaching of children.

Synagogue worship was doubtless very simple in its early history. The elements of prayer and the reading and explanation of a portion of Scripture were doubtless parts of the service from the earliest days. By the time of the Mishna (2nd and 3rd centuries after Christ) five principal parts of the service are enumerated: The Shema, prayer, the reading of the Law, the reading of the prophets with the benediction, and the translation and explanation of the Scripture lesson.

The Shema receives its name from the Hebrew word meaning "hear." It consists of Deuteronomy 6:4-9; 11:13-21; and Numbers 15:37-41. A benediction is uttered before and after the reading of the Shema. The reciting of the Shema doubtless stems from the desire of the pious in Israel to teach the sacredness and importance of the Law. Outward, symbolic signs known as frontlets (N.T. "phylacteries") are enjoined as reminders of God's Law. The opening words of the Shema were quoted by Jesus (Mark 12:29) in answer to the question, "Which commandment is the first of all?" The use of phylacteries and fringes is well known in the New Testament (cf. Matt. 23:5), giving evidence of the use of the Shema in the synagogue service during pre-Christian times. The conception of the Shema as a confession of faith and a substitute for animal sacrifices is a later development.

At the beginning of the second century the chief prayer of the synagogue was the *Shemoneh 'esreh,* "eighteen (benedictions)." These prayers traditionally are ascribed to the time of Ezra, with a final redaction around A.D. 110 by Rabbi Simeon ha-Pakkoli. In point of fact the New Testament does not give evidence of a fixed form of prayer. Great leaders and learned rabbis seem to have suggested suitable prayers which were adopted by their disciples. We are told that John the Baptist taught his disciples a form of prayer (Luke 11:1). The disciples asked Jesus to do likewise, and the Savior responded with the Lord's Prayer.

The present form of the *Shemoneh 'esreh* comes from the period subsequent to the fall of Jerusalem (A.D. 70). It exists in two different recensions, one from Palestine and the other from Babylon.

The reading of a lesson from the Law was the most prominent part of the synagogue service. Tradition says, "Moses instituted the reading of the Law on the sabbaths, feast-days, new moons, and half feast days; and Ezra appointed the reading of the Law for Mondays and Thursdays and the sabbath afternoons" (Jer. *Meg.* 75a). Actually the development of the reading of the Law went through a varied history. There were annual cycles for completing the reading of the Law, two-year cycles, three-, and three-and-a-half-year cycles in use at different times. These cycles were based on the consecutive reading of the Law, with portions assigned for both weekdays and sabbaths. Special readings were chosen for the four Sabbaths before passover, festivals, half-festivals, new moons, and fast days.

Every Israelite, even minors, could partake in the public reading of the Law. On the Sabbath day at least seven readers were chosen. If priests were present, they were called on first, followed by Levites, and then by lay members of the congregation. Special benedictions were pronounced by the first reader before the reading, and by the last reader at the end. After each verse an Aramaic rendering *(targum)* was given by an interpreter *(methurgeman)*. In Palestine the interpreters were not permitted to use written translations. They were required to adhere to the traditional rendering and to refrain from allegorizing.

The selection of a portion from the Prophets forms a further step in the development of the synagogue ritual. The readings from the Prophets seem to have been chosen with a view to the explanation or illustration of the Law. It is thought that the reading of prophetic portions had not yet been systematized by New Testament times, and that the selection read by Jesus in the synagogue of Nazareth (Luke 4:16) was his own choice. As in the case of the Law, an interpreter translated the lesson from the Prophets into Aramaic. He was permitted to translate three verses at a time from the prophetic portions.

Although the sermon was not an essential part of the synagogue service, the translation and explanation of the Scripture lesson was a step in the direction of a preaching service. There is evidence that an exposition of the lesson formed a part of the Sabbath afternoon service. In earliest times the sermon seems to have been connected with the reading from the Prophets. Anyone able to instruct might be asked to preach (Acts 13:15). The preacher spoke from a sitting position on an elevated place (Luke 4:20).

At the close of the service a blessing was pronounced by a priestly member of the congregation. All present responded with an Amen. If no priest or Levite was present, the blessing was made into a prayer.

The Building

Our knowledge of the synagogue buildings is derived from descriptions in ancient literature and the discovery of the ruins of ancient synagogues by archaeologists. The chief article of furniture in the synagogue was the "ark," containing the scrolls of the Law and other sacred writings. The ark stood by the wall farthest from the entrance. In the center of the synagogue was a raised platform (bemah), on which was placed a lectern. The rest of the room contained wooden seats. The chief seats were those nearest to the ark, facing the people. Since the Middle Ages, women have been assigned to the balconies of orthodox synagogues, but it is not at all certain that this was true in antiquity. There is evidence, on the contrary, that women could sit in the chief seats of the synagogue and bear titles of honor in the synagogue.

Probably the most spectacular synagogue discovery is that of Dura-Europus in Syria, excavated by M. I. Rostovtzeff of Yale from 1932-1935. Elaborate murals show such scenes as the resurrection of the dry bones described by Ezekiel, and the anointing of David.

As a rule the front of a synagogue faced Jerusalem, and contained three entrances. There was a desire to place the synagogue on the highest spot in the city. Proximity to water was desirable because of the necessity for ceremonial ablutions.

Most of our information on ancient synagogues comes from the period after the ministry of Jesus. It does exhibit, however, a variety which was hardly expected. Elaborate murals, mosaics with designs of lions, horses, goats, and different varieties of birds, elaborate Doric and Corinthian type pillars show a feeling for art which was earlier thought incompatible with Jewish loyalty to the Law which forbade "graven images." It may be unwise to generalize as the result of a limited number of synagogue discoveries, but it seems safe to say that varying attitudes existed among the Jews with reference to art in the synagogue. In some ages, and in some places, a very tolerant attitude prevailed. In other times, a rigorous attitude toward the Law resulted in iconoclastic movements.

Renan called the synagogue "the most original and fruitful creation of the Jewish people." As an institution it has been the rallying point of Judaism from the Babylonian exile to the present day. In Jewish synagagues Jesus spoke and Paul preached. The earliest Christian church adapted the synagogue type of service as the vehicle of Christian growth and evangelism. Without the development of the synagogue, neither Judaism nor Christianity could exist as we know them today.

part two

**The Hellenistic
Period**

8

ALEXANDER, THE APOSTLE OF HELLENISM

Since the days of Xerxes, Greek power had been on the increase and Persia had trouble in keeping its wide empire in submission. The city states of Greece, however, never formed a united government, and the wily Persian kings were able to play off one state against another.

When a real union of Greek states was achieved, it was the genius of Philip of Macedon — not, strictly speaking, a Greek at all — that brought it about. The Hellenic League, comprising all the Greek states except Sparta, became the instrument which gave the Persian Empire its death blow.

Philip was unable to bring his plans to fruition. He was murdered in 336 B.C., and his mantle fell on his young son Alexander. Like most great leaders, Alexander represented a mass of conflicting strands. He was a Macedonian by nationality, and he dreamed of national glory as the heir of Philip. Culturally he was a Greek, educated by Aristotle himself. He carried the *Iliad* and the *Odyssey* with him on his campaigns. Alexander was thoroughly sold on the excellences of the Greek "way of life," although the Greeks gave him little support. When the people of Thebes assassinated the Macedonian garrison, Alexander burned the city and sold its inhabitants into slavery. This was to serve as a warning that the "alliance" between the Greeks and Macedon must be respected.

The apostle of Hellenism made a very humble beginning. With a small army, largely of Macedonians, and a staff of historians, geographers, and botanists, Alexander crossed the Dardanelles by boat at the very spot where Xerxes had taken his army across on a carefully prepared bridge. Alexander captured Troy and sacrificed to the *manes* of the Greek heroes, thereby proclaiming the fact that a new war had begun.

The Persian sovereign, Darius III, did not take this expedition seriously. He ordered that Alexander be seized and brought to Susa. An army of Persian cavalry, Greek mercenaries, and native troops was sent by Darius to stop Alexander. Expecting an easy victory, the Persians clashed with Alexander at the river Granicus. It was a close fight, and Alexander nearly lost his life, but the Persians were defeated. Alexander did not pursue the retreating Persian cavalry, but he ordered the Greek mercenaries massacred as traitors to the Greek cause. With the victory at the Granicus, the way into Asia Minor lay open before Alexander.

The Greek cities of Asia Minor were taken and "liberated," in many instances against their will. Halicarnasus remained loyal to Persia, and was burned during a siege. Alexander was able to move eastward, conquering and organizing the districts that fell before him, with no serious challenge until he came to the Cilician Gates at Issus. Here Darius advanced with his Persian army to stop the Macedonian. Instead the Persians fell back before Alexander. Damascus was taken by surprise. The family of Darius, immense stores of booty, and ambassadors from Sparta, Athens, and Thebes were captured.

Alexander decided not to pursue Darius. Military tactics demanded that Alexander secure his rear. The Phoenician cities, except Tyre, surrendered and were occupied. On two occasions Darius offered to negotiate with Alexander, offering him territory, a large sum of money, and the hand of his daughter in marriage in return for the return of his family. By this time, however, Alexander had decided upon a policy of world conquest, and Darius' offer went unheeded.

The resistance of Tyre occupied Alexander for seven months. The persistence of Alexander is seen in the causeway which he built from the mainland city to the island city of Tyre, in order to bring the Tyrians into submission. The very map of Phoenicia was changed during this siege of Tyre. The city finally fell, and with the fall of Tyre the maritime and commercial predominance of the Phoenicians came to an end.

After a two month siege of Gaza, during which Alexander was wounded, the victorious Macedonians pressed on to Egypt. The Egyptians hated the Persians, and welcomed Alexander as a deliverer. Alexander entered the temple of Ammon where the oracle announced that Alexander was the son of Ammon and that he would conquer the world. The Hellenism of Alexander must have worn thin when he accepted the role of a son of Ammon, but he gladly did so, being recognized as a legitimate Pharaoh with a chapel in the temple at Karnak. The administration of Egypt was reorganized. Egyptians were given a large share of the control of their country, but Macedonians were placed in charge of the army. The new city of Alexandria was the enduring monument to the Macedonian conquest of Egypt. It replaced Tyre as the commercial metropolis of the eastern Mediterranean. Jewish colonists were encouraged to settle in Alexandria, and their presence there had an important bearing on the subsequent history of Judaism and Christianity.

Jewish traditions show Alexander in a friendly light, although Hellenism was to become the great enemy of orthodox Judaism. Josephus tells a story of Alexander's coming to Jerusalem and offering sacrifice in the Temple "according to the High-priest's direction." Although regarded as unhistorical, it shows the friendly attitude of the Jews to Alexander.

In 331 B.C., Alexander retraced his steps northward through Palestine and Syria. He now felt ready to meet the Persian army in its home territory. At the battle of Gaugamela, in the Mesopotamian plain, Alexander outmaneuvered and defeated the "Grand Army" of Darius. The Persian monarch escaped, however. With no army to impede his progress, Alexander marched on until he had taken the entire territory of Persia. The capitals of the Persian Empire — Babylon, Susa, Persepolis, and Ecbatana — were successively occupied.

The conquest of Babylon was reminiscent of the days of Cyrus. Alexander was welcomed as a liberator. The priests of Marduk and the nobles of the city brought gifts and promised to surrender the treasures of Babylon to Alexander. The garrison commander ordered flowers for the streets and crowns to honor the new Great King. Costly perfumes were burned on the altars. Magi chanted hymns. Alexander responded by ordering the rebuilding of temples which had lain waste since the days of Xerxes. The temple of Bel Marduk was to become the glory of Babylon again.

Twenty days after he left Babylon, Alexander entered Susa where the treasure of the palace of Darius I was his for the taking. Having plundered Susa, Alexander went on to Persepolis which was reported to be the richest city in the world. Historians are puzzled by the cruelty of Alexander at Persepolis. The men were all slain, and the women enslaved. The Macedonians fought one another over the plunder. By 330 B.C., Darius was dead, and Alexander assumed the title *Basileus*

(Great King). The sack of Persepolis was probably designed to mark the end of the Persian monarchy.

With the conquest of Persia behind him, Alexander continued his eastern conquests. Bactria and Sogdiana (Russian Turkestan) cost him three years of bitter fighting. As a gesture of reconciliation, Alexander married Roxana, a Bactrian princess. The Punjab region of India was the limit of Alexander's conquests. His army refused to travel further.

Alexander began his career as an apostle of Hellenism. Completely convinced that the Greek way of life was superior to any other, he began his crusade with a missionary zeal. When he was recognized in Egypt as a son of Ammon he took a major step away from Greek ideology. In Persia, Alexander decided to adopt Persian dress, and he began to rule as an oriental despot. A conspiracy against Alexander was said to implicate the son of one of his most able generals, Parmenion. Father and son were both put to death.

Tragedy crowned the last years of Alexander. Half of his army took the return trip from India in a navy of newly built ships. From the Indus Delta the fleet successfully made the voyage to the Persian gulf. The rest of the army traveled by land. In 324 Alexander arrived in Susa to find misrule on the part of the officials left in charge of the city. He also found that resentment to his own rule was growing. In Greece many were scandalized when they heard that Alexander had executed his own nephew, the historian Callisthenes. The Greeks were angered at the report that Alexander wished to be treated as a god. Alexander's Macedonian officers resented his commands to mingle with the Persians and take Persian wives. The orientalizing ways of Alexander resulted in a mutiny, which was put down.

In 323 B.C. Alexander planned a sea voyage around Arabia, but he died of a fever before the voyage was accomplished. He was only thirty-three years of age. His only son was born to Roxana after Alexander's death. In so short a life, Alexander conquered more territory than any of his predecessors. Although he had not had time to mold the government of his empire into a cohesive whole, the eleven years from the time that Alexander crossed the Dardanelles until his death in Babylon changed the course of history. Hellenism was to outlive its militant apostle.

9

THE JEWS UNDER THE PTOLEMIES

When Alexander died in 323 B.C., he left no heir. A son was posthumously born to Roxana, Alexander's Bactrian wife, but the *diadochoi,* or "successors" of Alexander, seized power before he could reach maturity. One of the *diadochoi,* Cassander, murdered Roxana and her son.

Alexander had had many able generals, but there was not one that arose as his logical successor. By 315 B.C., after seven years of struggle, four outstanding leaders appeared: Antigonus, who occupied the country from the Mediterranean to central Asia; Cassander, who ruled Macedonia; Ptolemy Lagi, who ruled Egypt and Southern Syria; and Lysimachus, ruler of Thrace. Ptolemy's foremost general was Seleucus who occupied an important role in the subsequent history of Palestine.

In 315 B.C., Ptolemy, Cassander, and Lysimachus formed an alliance to check Antigonus, who aspired in his own right to be a second Alexander. Ptolemy demanded that Antigonus yield part of the Asiatic territory which he had conquered. Seleucus was to receive Babylon, from which he had previously been driven out. When Antigonus failed to heed Ptolemy's demands, fighting broke out. Ptolemy and Seleucus defeated an army led by Demetrius, Antigonus' son, at Gaza in 312 B.C. They pressed on, taking the important Syrian cities, including Zidon.

Josephus quotes Agatharchides' account of Ptolemy's capture of Jerusalem:

"The people known as Jews, who inhabit the most strongly fortified of cities, called by the natives Jerusalem, have a custom of abstaining from work every seventh day; on those occasions they neither bear arms nor take any agricultural operations in hand, nor engage in any other forms of public service, but pray with outstretched hands in the temples until the evening. Consequently, because the inhabitants, instead of protecting their city, persevered in their folly, Ptolemy, son of Lagus, was allowed to enter with his army; the country was thus given over to a cruel master, and the defect of a practice enjoined by law was exposed. That experience has taught the whole world, except that nation, the lesson not to resort to dreams and traditional fancies about the law, until its difficulties are such as to baffle human reason."[1]

The *Letter of Aristeas* says of Ptolemy:

"He had overrun the whole of Coele-Syria and Phoenicia, exploiting his good fortune and prowess, and had transplanted some and made others captive, reducing all to subjection by terror; it was on this occasion that he transported a hundred thousand persons from the country of the Jews to Egypt. Of these he armed some thirty thousand chosen men and settled them in garrisons in the country."[2]

Egyptian inscriptions and papyri indicate the presence of large numbers of Jews in Ptolemaic Egypt. Some of these had come earlier, but there is no reason to doubt that large numbers were brought to Egypt by Ptolemy Lagi.

Our sources of information concerning life in Palestine during the century of Ptolemaic rule are very scanty. For the most part the Jews were permitted to live in peace and in accord with their religious and cultural traditions. There are no records of tyranny such as characterized the Seleucid rule of Antiochus Epiphanes. Tribute was paid to the Egyptian government, but local affairs were administered by the High Priests who had been entrusted with responsibility for the government of the Jews since Persian times.

The one great figure among the Jews of the Ptolemaic period is Simon the Just, the High Priest who is the subject of the highest praise in the post-Biblical writings. Ecclesiasticus calls him "great among his brethren and the glory of his people." He is credited with rebuilding the walls of Jerusalem which had been demolished by Ptolemy I. He is said to have repaired the Temple and directed the excavation of a great reservoir which would provide fresh water for Jerusalem even in times of drought or siege.

In addition to his office as High Priest and head of the community, Simon was reputed to be the chief teacher of the people. His favorite maxim was, "The world rests on three things, on the Law, on Divine Service, and on Charity."[3]

The identity of Simon the Just is a historical problem. Simon I lived during the middle of the third century, and Simon II lived around 200 B.C. One of these is doubtless the Simon the Just of Jewish tradition and legend.

Nothing is known about the High Priest Onias I, but the house of Onias and the house of Tobias were to become bitter

---

1. Josephus *Contra Apion* i. 209, 210.
2. *Aristeas to Philocrates*, 12-13. Translation of Moses Hadas.
3. *Pirke Aboth* i. 2.

rivals. The house of Tobias was pro-Egyptian and represented the wealthy class of Jerusalem society. The Tobiads may have been related to "Tobiah the Ammonite" who gave so much trouble to Nehemiah (Neh. 2:10, 4:3,7; 6:1-19). A papyrus from the time of Ptolemy II speaks of a Jew named Tobias who was a cavalry commander in the Ptolemaic army stationed in Ammanitis, east of the Jordan.[4] A third century B.C. mausoleum with Aramaic letters "Tobiah" was discovered at 'Araq el-Emir in central Jordan.

The Tobiads are thought to have been tax collectors, occupying the same function as the "publicans" of New Testament times.

Josephus states that Onias II refused to pay Ptolemy IV twenty talents of silver, which seems to have been a kind of tribute demanded of the High Priests. By refusing payment, Onias appeared to be renouncing allegiance to Ptolemy. Joseph, a member of the house of Tobias, thereupon succeeded in having himself appointed tax farmer for the whole of Palestine. The "tax farmer" had to go to Alexandria each year and bid for the renewal of the license to gather taxes. Joseph held this influential post for twenty years, under the Ptolemies and, after the victory of Antiochus III, under the Seleucids.

Ptolemy's triumph in Palestine was short-lived, for Antigonus promptly drove him out of Syria and held it firmly. Seleucus also gained strength as an independent conqueror, no longer subject to Ptolemy. Antigonus tried to check Seleucus, but was unable to do so. In 311 B.C. Seleucus conquered Babylonia, marking the beginning of the Seleucid dynasty. Antigonus, however, continued to hold Syria, which served as a wedge between the holdings of Ptolemy and Seleucus.

In 301 B.C. Lysimachus, Seleucus, and Cassander with their combined forces met and overcame the forces of the empire-conscious Antigonus at Ipsus, in Phrygia. Antigonus died on the battlefield, and his Asiatic empire came to an end, although his son Demetrius Poliorketes managed to retain Macedonia and the Phoenician coast of Syria.

Ptolemy had remained on the sidelines during the fighting at Ipsus. It had been agreed that Coele-Syria, or Palestine, would be assigned to Ptolemy in the event of victory over Antigonus. Since Ptolemy had not taken an active part in the fighting, the other three allies decided that the territory should be assigned

4. Zenon Papyri, No. 13 publication by C. C. Edgar, in *Annales Serv.*, Vol. xviii (1919).

to Seleucus. In the meantime, however, Ptolemy had taken possession of the land. Diodorus describes the problems involved:

> "When Seleucus, after the partition of the kingdom of Antigonus, arrived with his army in Phoenicia, and tried, according to the arrangements concluded, to take over Coele-Syria, he found Ptolemy already in possession of its cities. Ptolemy complained that Seleucus, in violation of their old friendship, should have agreed to an arrangement which put territory governed by Ptolemy into his own share. Although he (Ptolemy) had taken part in the war against Antigonus, the kings had not, he protested, assigned him any portion of the conquered territory. To these reproaches Seleucus replied that it was quite fair that those who fought the battle should dispose the territory. With regard to Coele-Syria, he would not, for the present, for the sake of friendship, take any action; later on he would consider the best way of treating friends who tried to grasp more than was their right."[5]

Syria was nominally a part of three domains after the battle of Ipsus. Demetrius Poliorketes, son of Antigonus, occupied the Phoenician coast. Seleucus possessed northern Syria where he built Antioch as his capital. Syria south of Aradus (Arvad) was retained by Ptolemy, who was able to encroach on the claims of his northern neighbors. While Demetrius was busy elsewhere, Ptolemy quietly occupied Phoenicia. Seleucus made no attempt to occupy Coele-Syria, so that Ptolemy remained its *de facto* ruler.

Ptolemy Lagi was succeeded by his son Ptolemy Philadelphus in 283 B.C. Seleucus was murdered in 281 B.C. and succeeded by his son Antiochus I. In the years that follow, three great powers shared the empire of Alexander. The Ptolemies of Egypt, the Seleucids of Syria, and the house of Antigonus in Macedonia were rival powers. The Seleucids and the Antigonids were either singly, or unitedly, at war with the Ptolemies during most of the third century B.C.

In 275 B.C. Ptolemy invaded Syria and was repulsed by the Seleucid forces. Ptolemy's naval power, however, enabled him to prolong the war. Hostilities ceased in 272 or 271 B.C. without a decisive victory for either side.

When Antiochus II succeeded his father to the Syrian throne in 261 B.C., war broke out again. The results were indecisive, and peace was concluded in 252 B.C. Ptolemy's daughter, Berenice, was betrothed to Antiochus II, thus uniting the two rival houses by marriage.

In 246 B.C. Antiochus died, being succeeded by his son Seleucus II. The following year Ptolemy II died and was succeeded by Ptolemy III, Euergetes, who had been joint-ruler since 247 B.C.

---

5. Diodorus, *Histories*, xxi, 5.

War broke out between the Seleucids and the Ptolemies when it was learned that Berenice had been murdered, with her infant son, through the intrigue of Laodice, half sister and wife of Antiochus II. Laodice wanted to insure that her own son, rather than the son of Berenice, would succeed to the Syrian throne. The murder of the daughter and grandson of Ptolemy II, however, was an outrage to the honor of the Ptolemies and resulted in the "Laodicean War."

After a series of brilliant victories in which northern Syria was completely subjugated, Ptolemy III was called back to Egypt to care for a local problem. Seleucus was able to regain lost territories as far south as Damascus, but attempts to take Southern Palestine were futile. Peace was concluded in 240 B.C., and no further attacks were made on Syria during Ptolemy III's reign. He died in 221 B.C. and was succeeded by Ptolemy IV Philopater, one of the worst of the Ptolemaic house. Seleucus II was succeeded, in 226, by Seleucus III who died by poison, according to Appian. He was succeeded by his younger brother who is known as Antiochus III, the Great.

10

THE JEWS UNDER THE SELEUCIDS

1. Antiochus III and the Conquest of Palestine

Antiochus III was only eighteen years of age when he came to the throne of Syria in 223 B.C. He had had experience in government, however, having served as ruler of Babylonia under his brother Seleucus III.

After crushing a revolt in the eastern part of his empire, Antiochus attempted to invade Coele-Syria in the summer of 221 B.C. He got as far as the fortresses of the Marsyas valley in Lebanon, but was forced to withdraw by Theodotus, the commander-in-chief of the Egyptian forces in Syria.

A second invasion was attempted in 219 B.C. with greater success. Seleucia in Pieria fell before Antiochus, and Theodotus transferred his loyalty from Ptolemy Philopater to Antiochus and delivered the cities of Ptolemais (Acre) and Tyre to the Syrians. Nicolaus, an Egyptian general, delayed Antiochus at the fortress of Dora, south of Mt. Carmel. When a rumor reached him that a strong Egyptian army was awaiting him at Pelusium, Antiochus accepted a truce and withdrew to Seleucia, leaving Theodotus in charge of the conquered territory. Sosibius, the Egyptian commander-in-chief, reorganized his army for a showdown.

Early in 218 B.C. Nicolaus marched with an Egyptian army to the Lebanons to meet the Syrians. Polybius describes the encounter:

> "When Theodotus had forced back the enemy at the foot of the mountain, and then charged from the higher ground, all those who were with Nicolaus turned and fled precipitately. About two thousand of them fell during the flight, and a not less number were captured; all the rest retreated on Zidon."[1]

Antiochus pursued the retreating army of Nicolaus down the Phoenician coast. Leaving Nicolaus in Zidon, Antiochus took

1. Polybius, *Histories*, v, 69.

Tyre and Ptolemais, then turned inland and came to Philoteria (Tiberias) on the Sea of Galilee. He crossed the Jordan taking the strong trans-Jordanian cities, including Gadara, and Philadelphia (Rabbath-Ammon). He returned to winter at Ptolemais.

In the spring of 217 B.C. Antiochus continued his conquests, conquering Philistia, including Gaza, before reaching the frontier town of Raphia. An Egyptian army under the personal command of Ptolemy Philopater met the Syrians south of Raphia. Here the armies of Antiochus met a disastrous defeat. Polybius says that Ptolemy "remained three months in Syria and Phoenicia setting things in order in the cities."[2]

The third book of Maccabees tells how Ptolemy visited the cities of Syria after his victory at Raphia. The Jews are alleged to have sent a group of elders to congratulate him on his victory. Ptolemy is reputed to have insisted on entering the Holy of Holies, only to flee in confusion and terror when he had gotten as far as the Holy Place (III Maccabees 1:9-11, 24). The story cannot be regarded as historical. It is significant that nothing is said of the incident in Daniel 11, which describes the incident at Raphia in considerable detail.

For a number of years Antiochus was busy in the East, but he never gave up his plans for annexing Coele-Syria to his domains. At the death of Ptolemy IV, Philopater, in 203 B.C., Egypt was rent with turmoil and rebellion. In the spring of 202 B.C. Antiochus launched an attack which accomplished little or nothing. The following spring another attack was launched, with bitter fighting in the Palestinian cities, including Gaza. Scopas, the Egyptian general, pushed the Syrians back to the sources of the Jordan during the winter of 201-200 B.C.

The decisive Syrian victory came at the Battle of Panion, near the sources of the Jordan. Scopas fled to Zidon where he was besieged by land and sea. In the spring of 198 B.C. Scopas was forced to surrender, leaving the whole of Syria in the hands of Antiochus. In passing through his newly acquired territories, Antiochus came to Jerusalem where, according to Josephus, the inhabitants gave him a cordial welcome.

When the Carthaginian, Hannibal, was defeated by the Romans at Zama (202 B.C.), bringing to an end the Second Punic War, he fled eastward and took refuge in the court of Antiochus. Still interested in stirring up trouble for Rome, he encouraged Antiochus to invade Greece. Rome thereupon declared war on Antiochus.

---

2. Polybius, *Histories*, v, 86, 87.

The Roman forces moved into Greece, defeated Antiochus, and forced him to retreat to Asia Minor. There at Magnesia, between Sardis and Smyrna, the Romans under Cornelius Scipio defeated Antiochus (190 B.C.). He had to pay an enormous indemnity, surrender his war elephants and his navy. The younger son of Antiochus the Great, later to rule as Antiochus Epiphanes, was taken to Rome as a hostage for the payment of the indemnity. His twelve years in Rome gave him a healthy respect for Roman power and Roman ways of doing things.

2. Antiochus Epiphanes and the Persecution of the Jews

The fall of Palestine into Syrian hands, following the victory of Antiochus the Great at Panion (198 B.C.), ushered in a new era of Jewish history. The rule of the Ptolemies had been tolerant. The Seleucids determined to force the Jews to accept Hellenism.

Antiochus IV bore the surname Epiphanes ("the illustrious," almost a title of deity). The Jews, masters of innuendo, gave him the nickname, Epimanes ("the madman"). He was born in Athens, and had served as chief magistrate of the city whose culture was the epitome of everything Greek. Antiochus spent twelve years as a hostage in Rome, where he learned to respect the new power which was about to conquer the world. With a sense of mission coupled with political astuteness, Antiochus determined "to civilize," which meant "to Hellenize," the domain over which he ruled.

It is possible to misrepresent Antiochus. He was not a foreigner intent on enslaving a persecuted minority group. On the contrary, a sizable number of Jews were impressed with the possibilities of greater conformity to the Hellenistic manners and customs. Antiochus used this inner dissension among the Jews, coupled with his own need of funds, to interfere in the internal affairs of Judea.

In the early days of the reign of Antiochus IV, Jerusalem was ruled by the High Priest, Onias III, a descendant of Simon the Just, and a strictly orthodox Jew. The Jews who looked favorably on Greek culture opposed Onias and espoused the cause of his brother, Jason. By promising larger tribute to Antiochus, Jason succeeded in having himself appointed High Priest.

To Antiochus, the high priesthood was a political office. As Syrian king, he would have the right to appoint whomever he chose. To the pious Jews, however, the priesthood was of divine origin, and its sale to the highest bidder was looked upon as a sin against God. Since the priesthood involved both civil and religious functions, both viewpoints would appear valid to their respective adherents.

Jason encouraged the Hellenists who had sought his election. A gymnasium was built in Jerusalem. There Jewish lads exercised in the nude in accord with Greek custom. Greek names were adopted in place of the more pious-sounding Jewish names. Hebrew orthodoxy was looked upon as obscurantist and obsolete. Antiochus visited Jerusalem in 170 B.C. He showed his approval of the new order of things by authorizing the citizens to call themselves "Antiochites" after their sovereign.

With the developing tide of Hellenism, however, there developed a resistance movement. The Hasidim (the "pious") followed the paths of their fathers and attempted a defense of orthodox Jewish institutions.

Antiochus, who was having trouble elsewhere in his empire, looked upon Jewish orthodoxy as a divisive force. Aiming at a united Hellenistic empire, he awaited an opportunity to implement his program.

Such an opportunity came when a dispute arose between Jason and one of his closest associates. Menelaus was of the tribe of Benjamin. As such, he had no right to the priestly office. Nevertheless, by offering higher tribute to Antiochus than that paid by Jason, he was nominated to the office of High Priest. A Syrian garrison was stationed in the citadel in Jerusalem to insure order and respect for the new High Priest.

If the Hasidim were scandalized when Jason replaced his brother Onias, they were infuriated when a Benjamite, who was a thoroughgoing Hellenist, was installed by force of Syrian arms.

The deposed Jason did not quietly acquiesce in the change. Unable, for the time being, to resist the forces of Antiochus, he awaited an opportunity to reassert himself.

Several years after Menelaus became High Priest, while Antiochus was busy fighting in Egypt, Jason raised an army in Transjordan and raided Jerusalem. Menelaus beat off the attack, but it became obvious to Antiochus that large segments of Judaism were still opposed to Hellenism and Syrian control in Palestine.

On the return of Antiochus from Egypt, Menelaus welcomed him to Jerusalem. What was left of the Temple treasure was placed at his disposal. Since Menelaus was unpopular with many of the Jews, he found it all the more necessary to court the favor of Antiochus.

During a second campaign in Egypt, Antiochus came as close

as he ever came to subduing the empire of the Ptolemies. He was deterred by the rise of a new power which was soon to transform the Mediterranean into a Roman lake.

At the Battle of Pydna (168 B.C.) the Romans defeated the Macedonians in one of history's decisive battles. On the ruins of the Macedonian empire, Rome was to make a name for herself. In his younger days Antiochus had come to know and respect the Romans. Rome was not ready to annex Syria and Egypt, but Rome was determined that Antiochus should not strengthen himself by annexing Egypt. In a famous scene outside the city of Alexandria, the Roman envoy demanded that Antiochus, before he stirred from a circle drawn around him in the ground, promise to evacuate Egypt. With dreams of grandeur suddenly dissipated, Antiochus turned back in bitterness.

If Egypt was to remain a rival power, Antiochus found it more necessary than ever to retain his hold on Palestine. He sent Appolonius, his general, to occupy the city of Jerusalem. In a Sabbath attack, when he knew that the orthodox Jews would not fight, he slaughtered large numbers of the opponents of Menelaus. The city walls were destroyed, and a new fortress, the Akra, was built on the site of the citadel. The Akra was garrisoned by a large force which was expected to keep the Jews in submission to the policies of Antiochus.

One of Israel's darkest periods began. A systematic attempt was made to Hellenize the country by force. An edict demanded the fusion of all the nationalities of the Seleucid empire into one people. Greek deities were to be worshiped by all.

An elderly Athenian philosopher was sent to Jerusalem to supervise the enforcement of the order. He identified the God of Israel with Jupiter, and ordered a bearded image of the pagan deity, perhaps in the likeness of Antiochus, set up upon the Temple altar. The Jews popularly spoke of this as "the Abomination of Desolation."

Greek soldiers and their paramours performed licentious heathen rites in the very Temple courts. Swine were sacrificed on the altar. The drunken orgy associated with the worship of Bacchus was made compulsory. Conversely, Jews were forbidden, under penalty of death, to practice circumcision, Sabbath observance, or the observance of the feasts of the Jewish year. Copies of the Hebrew Scriptures were ordered destroyed.

These laws promulgating Hellenism and proscribing Judaism were enforced with the utmost cruelty. An aged Scribe, Eleazar, was flogged to death because he refused to eat swine's flesh. A mother and her seven children were successively butchered, in the presence of the governor, for refusing to pay homage to an image. Two mothers who had circumcised their new-born sons were driven through the city and cast headlong from the wall. Later ages may have exaggerated the atrocities of Antiochus, but there is no possibility of seeing him as anything but an oppressor who merited the name Epimanes — the Madman.

By force of arms the Hellenizing party had gained a victory. Menelaus continued as High Priest. Where once his worship was directed to Yahweh, the God of Israel, now he served Jupiter. Yet the Hellenizers had gone too far. Their very zeal for a quick defeat of the "old order" evoked a reaction which drove the Hellenizers out of power and brought into being an independent Jewish state.

11

THE IMPACT OF HELLENISM ON THE JEWS

Alexander the Great had been a missionary as well as a conqueror. From his teacher Aristotle he had been taught the virtues of Greek philosophy and the Greek "way of life." Although his journeys toward the east caused him to adopt non-Greek practices, and a Greek purist would be shocked at his assumption of the role of a deity, Alexander continued to think of himself as one who was bringing the blessings of Hellenism, as the Greek way of life is called, to more benighted parts of the world. Alexander had attempted to establish a model Hellenistic community in each of the lands he had conquered. Alexandria in Egypt is the best known and most successful of these planned communities. Alexander was sure that the excellences which these communities represented would have the effect of making Hellenism attractive to the countries in which they were located.

Although the empire of Alexander was short lived, being divided shortly after his death, his cultural accomplishments were of much longer duration. In the years following Alexander's death, Palestine was subject successively to the Egyptian Ptolemies and the Syrian Seleucids, but in each case the culture was Hellenistic. Although military rivals, culturally the states which emerged from the empire of Alexander were one. The city-states of mainland Greece became stagnant during the three pre-Christian centuries, but Hellenistic centers such as Alexandria, Pergamum, and Dura became centers of cultural activity.

The Hellenistic city could readily be identified. Fine public buildings were erected. A gymnasium was built for that culture of the body which the Greeks always stressed. An open air theater was built to entertain the populace. Greek dress was observed in the city, with people speaking the Greek language and subscribing to one of the schools of Greek philosophy. The city government was modeled along the lines of the Greek city-states.

Hellenism was not all bad, or all good. It did, however, present a challenge to Judaism both in the "dispersion" and in Palestine proper. Norman Bentwich observes, "The interaction of Judaism and Hellenistic culture is ... one of the fundamental struggles in the march of civilization ..."[1] If the great temptation to pre-exilic Israel was the idolatry of its Canaanite neighbors, the great temptation of post-exilic Judaism was Hellenistic attitudes toward life.

1. Hellenism in the Dispersion

General Influence

At no time after the Babylonian exile did the majority of Jews live in Palestine. Many remained in their settlements in Babylon, or settled in other parts of the Tigris-Euphrates valley. Others went to Syria where there were large Jewish settlements, particularly in Antioch and Damascus. Asia Minor had large Jewish communities. Lydia, Phrygia, Ephesus, Pergamum, and Sardis all had numerous Jews in their population. The account of the visitors to Jerusalem on the day of Pentecost (Acts 2) and the journeys of the apostle Paul give us a significant picture of the settlements of the Jews of the dispersion. These Jews remained loyal to the Jerusalem Temple. Every male Israelite over the age of twenty was expected to pay his Temple dues, and pilgrimages were made whenever possible. Each settlement, however, took on something of the characteristics of its neighbors, so that the Jews of Babylon would not have the same attitudes as those of Egypt. Those of Palestine would be apt to consider themselves alone the truly orthodox.

The most significant group of Jews of the dispersion, historically speaking, was that of Alexandria. From the initial settlement of Alexandria the Jews had formed one of the most important and largest segments of the city. Here was the temptation to assimilate to the prevailing Hellenistic pattern, and here also was the determination to remain true to the faith. A third century B.C. writer, Hecataeus of Abdera, wrote, "In recent times under the foreign rule of the Persians, and then of the Macedonians by whom the Persian Empire was overthrown, intercourse with other races has led to many of the traditional Jewish ordinances losing their hold."[2]

1. Norman Bentwich, *Hellenism*, p. 11.
2. E. R. Bevan, *Jerusalem Under the High Priests*, p. 43.

The nature of the temptation which beset the Jews in the midst of Hellenism may be noted from the writings of the ancient historian Posidonius:

"The people of these cities are relieved by the fertility of their soil from a laborious struggle for existence. Life is a continuous series of social festivities. Their gymnasiums they use as baths where they anoint themselves with costly oils and myrrhs. In the *grammateia* (such is the name they give to the public eating-halls) they practically live, filling themselves there for the better part of the day with rich foods and wine; much that they cannot eat they carry away home. They feast to the prevailing music of strings. The cities are filled from end to end with the noise of harp-playing."[3]

Even for those who might not be tempted by such a prospect of a life of ease, there were other aspects of Hellenism that seemed to offer a fuller life than the older ways. The merchant class was able to amass great wealth which could purchase better housing and food than the pre-Hellenistic world could have imagined. Great libraries in Alexandria and other Hellenistic centers, together with schools emphasizing a Greek education, would appeal to many of the nobler youths of Israel. Sculpture and the fine arts offered an aesthetic outlook which would be frowned upon by the orthodox, but which would make an impact on the young in particular. In Alexandria a synthesis developed between Judaism and Hellenism.

The Septuagint

The greatest monument of Alexandrian Judaism was, without question, the translation of the Hebrew Old Testament into the Greek vernacular. While the origin of this version is unknown, legend places the beginning of this translation in the reign of the first of the Ptolemies (Philadelphus). While the legends suggest that the work was done in order to provide a copy of the Hebrew Scriptures for the Alexandrian library, it is more likely that the translation was made at the impulse of Alexandrian Jews who wanted their Greek-speaking children to be able to read the Scriptures. As the mother tongue (Hebrew) was forgotten by the younger generation, some provision had to be made for the preservation of the Hebrew sacred literature in the popularly spoken Greek. The Torah, or Pentateuch, was translated sometime around 250 B.C. The remainder of the canonical books of the Old Testament were subsequently translated, as were the apocryphal books. By the time of Origen (third century A.D.) this entire collection was called "the Septuagint," although the term originally referred

---

3. *Ibid.* p. 43 f.

only to the Greek translation of the Pentateuch. That a copy found its way into the library need not be doubted.

Around 100 B.C. a letter known as the *Letter of Aristeas* was written to describe the way in which the Septuagint was produced. This letter purports to have been written by an official in the court of Ptolemy Philadelphus of Egypt (285-246 B.C.). Philadelphus was an enlightened ruler who distinguished himself as a patron of the arts. Under him the great Library of Alexandria, one of the cultural wonders of the world for almost a millennium, was inaugurated. It was for Ptolemy Philadelphus that Manetho compiled his great history of Egypt which divided the history of Egypt into thirty dynasties. Although inaccurate in many places, Manetho's divisions are still used today.

According to the *Letter of Aristeas,* Demetrius of Phalerum, said to have been Ptolemy's librarian, aroused the king's interest in the Jewish Law. At his suggestion, Ptolemy sent a delegation to the High Priest, Eleazar, in Jerusalem, who chose six elders from each of the twelve tribes to translate the Law into Greek. These seventy-two elders, with a specially accurate and beautiful copy of the Law, were sent to Alexandria where they proved their fitness for their important task. They were sent to the island of Pharos, famed for its lighthouse, where, according to the Letter of Aristeas, in seventy-two days they completed their translation work and presented a version which they all agreed upon. The story was later embellished with the idea that the seventy-two were sent into individual cells, each translating the whole Law, all versions agreeing exactly when compared with one another after seventy-two days!

There can be no doubt that the legends which have been advanced concerning the origin of the Septuagint were designed to prove that it was an inspired and authoritative translation. When Jerome went behind the Septuagint to the Hebrew Old Testament, he was censured by many of his contemporaries who looked upon the Septuagint as the official Bible of the church in the fourth century.

Although the legends contained in the *Letter of Aristeas* cannot be believed, they do reflect a belief that the Law was translated into Greek during the time of Philadelphus. There is evidence that this is correct. Quotations from the Septuagint text of Genesis and Exodus appear in Greek literature before 200 B.C. The language of the Septuagint, however, suggests that it was made by Egyptian Jews rather than Jerusalemite elders. The story contained in the *Letter of Aristeas* evidently had a specific propaganda purpose. As numerous translations appeared, there was a desire to make one superior version definitive. If it could be proved that the Septuagint had been inspired in the same sense as the Hebrew originals, then the Greek-speaking Jew would have an infallible authority comparable to that of his Palestinian brother.

Although without question translated by Alexandrian Jews for their own use, the Septuagint did serve as a means of acquainting the non-Jew with the principles of Jewish faith and practice. No doubt a copy was placed in the famous Alexandrian library. When we come to New Testament times, we read of many "God-fearers" among the gentiles. In a real sense the Septuagint helped to pave the way for the ministry of the apostle Paul and others who took the message of Christ to non-Jew as well as to Jew. The Biblical preaching in the Greek-speaking world was based on the Septuagint text. Many of the New Testament quotations from the Old are taken from the Septuagint, although others are translated from the Hebrew and others do not accord perfectly with either the Hebrew or Greek texts which we know. In most, if not all, of these cases the writers are apparently paraphrasing the Scripture which they assume to be known to their readers.

Alexandrian Allegorism

With no intention to abandon their ancestral faith, Alexandrian Jews followed their gentile neighbors in subscribing to a school of Greek philosophy. This resulted in that attempt to harmonize Scripture with Greek thinking which produced the allegorical method of interpreting Scripture. Aristobulus and Philo were the great allegorizers. To them the literal meaning of the Bible was vulgar, misleading, and insufficient. A hidden, deeper meaning must be sought. By reading into the Bible their pagan philosophy, they were able to consider themselves enlightened Hellenists and orthodox Hebrews at one and the same time. Some of them adopted Greek names to help in the process of assimilation.

The allegorist regards the literal sense of Scripture as the vehicle for a secondary sense which is regarded as more spiritual and profound. The method is associated with the name of Origen, one of the early Church Fathers. As a method of Biblical interpretation it is rejected by careful scholars, but vestiges of it do appear in the extreme typology which is still prevalent in some circles.

Allegorism is of Greek origin. With the development of a philosophical and historical tradition which appealed to the thinking man, a serious problem was raised. Homer's *Iliad* and *Odyssey*, and Hesiod's *Theogany* contained ideas which the sophisticated Greek could no longer seriously accept. Yet these writings were cultural and religious classics. Was there no way in which they might be preserved?

The Stoics produced a solution. The stories of the gods, their lust and jealousy, their drunkenness and revelry, should not be accepted as historical truth. These stories really illustrated the struggle among the virtues. Zeus became the Logos ("Word" or "Idea"). Hermes represented Reason. Once such a "key" was developed to explain the "real" meaning of the classical epics, the Greek felt secure both in his ancient epic-religious heritage and his modern philosophical-historical attitude. Through allegorical interpretation the Alexandrian Greeks preserved their religious literature from oblivion by making it mean what it certainly was never intended to mean.

The Alexandrian Jew took a lesson from his Greek neighbor. As a loyal Jew he looked upon his Bible as the Word of God. He loved his Jewish faith with its religious observances and emphasis on the faithfulness of God and His call to Abraham and his descendants. Yet the Alexandrian Jew was more than a son of Abraham. He was also an heir to the culture of Greece as that culture had been spread abroad by Alexander. There was much in Hellenism that he esteemed. The Alexandrian Jew wanted to be a child of his times as much as the Alexandrian Greek did, and he used similar means.

Convinced that he could be a faithful Jew and a consistent Hellenist, the Alexandrian decided to accept a Greek philosophy and apply the allegorical method to bring harmony between the two. About 160 B.C. an Alexandrian Jew named Aristobulus taught that the Greek philosophers had actually borrowed much of their thought from the Mosaic Law. To Aristobulus, Moses and the prophets presented the same truths as those enunciated by the great Greek philosophers.

The most famous name in Jewish allegorical thought is Philo, the son of a wealthy Alexandrian merchant, who lived from about 20 B.C. to about A.D. 50. A man of great erudition, Philo mentions sixty-four Greek writers, including Homer, Hesiod, Pindar, Solon, the tragedians, and Plato. To Philo, these Greeks were not heathen. They were men of God, on a par with Israel's prophets. From Pythagoras, Plato, Aristotle, and the Stoics, Philo was able to weave for himself a philosophical system. Moses was looked upon as the greatest thinker of all. The lesser sages had all learned from him, and all truth could be found in the Law of Moses. Philo recognized that this was not always apparent in the letter. Under the letter of the Law, however, it could be found by using allegorical interpretation.

Philo regarded himself as a thoroughly orthodox Jew. He may not have known the Hebrew language at all, but he accepted the Greek Septuagint Version as a mechanically inspired volume. In his Septuagint he determined to find the "true" or allegorical sense. The literal sense might be tame, or even absurd, but the "true" sense could be learned by applying certain basic principles.

Allegorical interpretation is thoroughly subjective. If the literal sense of Scripture suggested something which the interpreter deemed unworthy of God, he considered this sufficient warrant to seek a "hidden" allegorical meaning. Anything deemed impossible or contrary to reason was allegorized. Anthropomorphism was offensive to the Greek mentality, so all references to God which imply human characteristics were eliminated by means of the allegorical concept. Abraham's journey to Palestine is made to be the story of a Stoic philosopher who leaves Chaldea (sensual understanding) and stops for a time at Haran ("holes" or "the senses"). Abraham's marriage to Sarah is the marriage of the philosopher to "abstract wisdom."

Considerable attention was paid to the form of Scripture. Any repetition in Scripture was interpreted as pointing to something new. If one of several possible synonymous words was chosen in a passage of Scripture, this pointed to some special meaning. A word in the Septuagint might be interpreted according to every shade of meaning it bore in Greek. By slightly altering the letters, still other meanings might be derived.

From the Jewish allegorists, the Christian church adopted a method of Biblical interpretation which has persisted in some places to the present. From the time of Origen it dominated the thinking of the Roman church. In antiquity there were notable exceptions, however. The Syrian school of Antioch, including such writers as Theodore of Mopsuestia, insisted on a literal interpretation of Scripture. Syria was removed from the influence of Alexandria, and showed a feeling for the true nature of Scripture, as over against allegorizing tendencies.

The reformation brought a renewed emphasis on the literal, historical interpretation of Scripture.

Summary

From the Christian point of view the Judaism of the dispersion served an important function. The translation of the Bible into Greek provided the church with a mighty weapon in its first contacts with the Greek-speaking gentile world. The Jewish communities were centers from which the gospel could be preached, during the lifetime of the apostle Paul, throughout the empire. The attempt to interpret Scripture allegorically and to form a synthesis between Biblical revelation and Greek speculative thought proved a snare to the early church. Under Origen, allegorical interpretation became the norm of Biblical study and remained such, with notable exceptions, until the Reformation in the sixteenth century.

2. Hellenism in Palestine

Palestine itself was not so far removed from the centers of Hellenism as to be untouched. Especially the educated classes were enamored with the Greek way of doing things. The amphitheater and the gymnasium were attractive to the young, and a strong Hellenistic party emerged.

In Judea, however, the lines were more closely drawn than they were in the dispersion. An anti-Hellenistic party arose which considered the Greek manner of life a threat to Judaism. The emphasis on things material, the nude appearance of athletes in the gymnasium, the neglect of Jewish rites, were regarded as evidence of defection from the law of God. The Hasidim, or "the pious," were ready to defend their ancestral faith to the death if need be, and in the days of Antiochus Epiphanes many of them did die for that faith. Future history shows us how necessary the Hasidim were in maintaining the place of the Law of the Lord in a day of moral and spiritual decay. A generation that was tempted to accept the worst aspects of Hellenistic life needed the corrective of a vibrant Hasidism.

12

THE MACCABEES AND THE STRUGGLE AGAINST HELLENISM

The oppressions of the Jews by Antiochus Epiphanes produced a reaction which stunned Antiochus and surprised many of the Jews themselves. The Hasidim needed but a leader. From the obscure village of Modin one emerged.

1. Mattathias

The emissaries of Antiochus erected a pagan altar at Modin. In order to show their loyalty to the government, the Jews were asked to come forward and sacrifice at the altar. The aged priest of the village, Mattathias, was asked to come forward first to set a good example for the others. Mattathias refused to sacrifice at the pagan altar. Fearing the wrath of Antiochus, a timid Jew made his way to the altar. Mattathias was enraged. He approached the altar, slew the apostate Jew and the emissary of Antiochus. With his five sons, Mattathias destroyed the heathen altar and fled to the hills to avoid the certain reprisals which might be expected from Antiochus. Others joined the family of Mattathias.

The early days of the Maccabean revolt, as the struggle against Antiochus and Hellenism came to be called, were days of guerrilla warfare. From their mountain strongholds, the sons of Mattathias and their allies raided the towns and villages, killing the royal officers and the Hellenistic Jews who supported them. A religious factor, however, favored the Syrians. Religious scruples kept the Maccabees from fighting on the Sabbath. On one Sabbath, a band of Maccabees was surrounded and slaughtered. They would not defend themselves. Sensing the gravity of the situation, Mattathias adopted the principle that fighting in self-defense was permissible even on the Sabbath day.

2. Judas the Maccabee

Soon after the beginning of the revolt, Mattathias died. He

urged his followers to choose as military leader his third son Judas (Hebrew, *Judah*), known as "the Maccabee" (usually interpreted as "the hammer"). Continuing victories in guerrilla warfare proved the choice a good one. More and more Jews rallied to the banner of Judas.

In the early days of the revolt the Syrians underestimated the strength of the Maccabees. Thinking the revolt only a minor skirmish, they sent inferior generals and small detachments of soldiers into the field. The Maccabees, however, were able to hold their own. They defeated one after another of the Syrian armies thrown against them.

Before long Antiochus realized that he had a full-sized rebellion on his hands. Because of its proximity to Egypt, Judea was particularly important. Yet Antiochus could not throw his full strength into Judea because he was faced with another revolt in Parthia at the same time. Antiochus moved eastward to Parthia, leaving his general Lysias to take care of the revolt in Judah.

Lysias sent an army of Syrians, Hellenistically minded Jews, and volunteers from the neighboring countries to defeat the Maccabean rebels. Nicanor and Gorgias, subordinates of Lysias, were in charge of the engagement. Judas, however, by a surprise night attack, annihilated the Syrian army and seized enormous stores of booty. This victory at the town of Emmaus opened the road to Jerusalem to the Maccabees.

Judas and his army moved on toward Jerusalem. Menelaus and his sympathizers fled. The Maccabees entered the city and were able to take everything except the fort known as the Akra. They entered the Temple and removed all of the signs of paganism which had been installed there. The altar dedicated to Jupiter was taken down and a new altar was erected to the God of Israel. The statue of Zeus-Antiochus was ground to dust. Beginning with the twenty-fifth of Kislev (December) they observed an eight-day Feast of Dedication, known as Hanukkah, or the Festival of Lights. In this way they celebrated the end of the three-year period during which the Temple had been desecrated.

Peace was short-lived, however. The neighboring lands had been sympathetic with the Syrians and had constantly harassed the Jews. Lysias, himself, marched against the Maccabees and defeated them in a battle near Jerusalem. He next besieged Jerusalem, hoping to starve the Maccabees into submission. During his siege, however, he learned that a rival was marching against Antioch, the capital of Syria. Anxious to head north, Lysias made an offer of peace to the Jews.

In the name of Syria, Lysias offered to refrain from interference in the internal affairs of Judea. Laws against the observance of Judaism would be repealed. Menelaus was to be removed from office, and the high priesthood given to a certain Jakim or Eliakim, better known by his Greek name of Alcimus. In this way a mild Hellenizer was to be recognized as High Priest. Lysias promised that Judas and his followers would not be punished. The walls of Jerusalem were to be razed, however.

These terms of peace were considered by the council at Jerusalem, a kind of provisional government. This council included the Maccabean army officers and the respected scribes and elders associated with the Hasidim, the party of orthodox Jews which had supported Judas.

The goal of the Hasidim had been religious liberty. This goal seemed to be in sight. Judas was not satisfied with anything short of full political as well as religious liberty. However, the appeal of a combination of peace and religious freedom won the day. The Hasidim had achieved their goal, and they were able to outvote the followers of Judas. The peace terms were accepted. Alcimus was installed as High Priest. Menelaus was executed. Judas and a few of his followers left the city.

The fears of Judas proved to be correct. Alcimus had a number of the Hasidim seized and executed. Many loyal Jews turned to Judas again and the civil war was renewed. This time, however, Judas was faced with more formidable opposition. Alcimus appealed to Syria for aid, and a sizable army was sent. The Hellenizing Jews adopted a more moderate attitude and won over large segments of the followers of Judas. Left with an ill-equipped army of eight hundred men, Judas bravely met the large Syrian army. He died in battle, ending the first phase of the Maccabean struggle.

3. Jonathan

Simon, Jonathan, and Johanan, brothers of Judas, with several hundred Maccabean soldiers, fled across the Jordan. From the standpoint of Syria they were a band of outlaws. To many of the Jews, however — even those who had made their peace with Alcimus — they were the true patriots. Jonathan became the leader of the band, and young Jews were constantly being attracted to their ranks. Syrian attempts to destroy this band of patriots were uniformly unsuccessful.

Victory finally came to Jonathan by diplomacy rather than

by war. When a pretender, Alexander Balas, claimed the Syrian throne of Demetrius II, both parties sought help from the Jews. They turned to Jonathan as the man best able to raise and lead a Jewish army, bypassing the Hellenistic Jews. Jonathan had no interest in either the pretender or Demetrius, who had tried to destroy him several times. He played a delaying action which proved successful. He supported Balas and made treaties with Sparta and Rome. Before the war was over, Jonathan was High Priest, governor of Judea, and a member of the Syrian nobility. Jonathan's brother Simon was governor of the Philistine coastal area.

Since both Judah and Rome were hostile to Syria, an alliance seemed desirable. The Roman senate declared itself the "Friend" of Judah, but no efforts were made to implement the declaration. In time, of course, Rome was to prove as much of an enemy as Syria.

Jonathan's foreign policy promoted the internal prosperity of Judah. The coastal cities, ruled by Simon, were practically annexed. When Judah died at the hand of a Syrian general, his brother Simon succeeded him as ruling High Priest.

4. Simon

Simon was advanced in years when he assumed office. Syria was again rent between two factions, one looking to Demetrius II as king, and the other recognizing the legitimacy of Antiochus VI, a boy under the guardianship of Tryphon. This Tryphon deposed Antiochus "and reigned in his stead, and put on him the diadem of Asia" (I Maccabees 13:31-32). Tryphon was the first Syrian king who was not of the Seleucid line. Simon ignored him, recognizing Demetrius as rightful king in Syria. Demetrius, in return, granted the Jews full immunity from taxes. This was interpreted as an acknowledgement of independence, and occasioned great rejoicing among the Jews. Simon was also able to starve out the Syrian garrison at the Akra and to occupy the cities of Joppa and Bethsura.

During the period of peace which marked the high priesthood of Simon, the question of the legitimacy of the Maccabean priests was settled. The Hasidic party recognized the line of Onias as the legitimate heirs to the Aaronic priesthood. The family of Onias had gone to Egypt during the Maccabean conflict, however, and any claims they had to the priesthood were thereby forfeited. In recognition of his wise rule, a convocation of the leaders in Israel named Simon "leader and High Priest for ever, until there should arise a faithful prophet" (I Maccabees 14:25-49).

This act legitimized a new dynasty which is known in history as the Hasmoneans. The name is thought to be derived from an ancestor of the Maccabeans named Asmonaeus, or (in Hebrew) Hashmon. Simon was the last of the sons of Mattathias. Under him, however, the concept of a hereditary high priesthood in the Hasmonean family was legitimized.

In 134 B.C., Simon and two of his sons were murdered by an ambitious son-in-law. A third son, John Hyrcanus, managed to escape. He succeeded his father as hereditary head of the Jewish state.

13

THE HASMONEAN DYNASTY, GROWTH AND DECAY

1. John Hyrcanus

With the death of the last of the sons of Mattathias, in 135 B.C., the heroic age of the Maccabean struggle came to an end. The generation which had fought for religious liberty was dying out. The new generation was proud of the Maccabean victories and hopeful of even greater successes at home and abroad.

Syria had to respect the leadership of her neighbor to the south. Although powerful enough to conquer Jerusalem, she offered recognition to Hyrcanus on condition that Hyrcanus consider himself subject to Syria and promise help in Syrian military campaigns. Hyrcanus was also asked to give up the coastal cities which had been annexed by his father and Jonathan. He was permitted to keep Jaffa which served as the port of Judah. The Syrian king left Palestine, and the Hellenizing party disappeared from the Jewish political scene.

This change in political alignments is an important factor in the reign of Hyrcanus. Previously the lines were closely drawn. The Hasidim represented the conservative elements who wished to retain their religious liberty and resist Hellenism. The Hellenizers were willing to sacrifice their religious heritage in order to achieve the real or imaginary gains included in the concept of "the Greek way of life." The Maccabean struggle resulted in victory for the Hasidim, although the Hasidim did not wholly align themselves with the Maccabees. They were willing to stop short of political independence in their dealings with the Syrians.

With the recognition of the government of Hyrcanus by the Syrians, the older Hellenists were completely discredited. Their conflict with the Hasmoneans was ended, and they became loyal members of the Jewish community.

The adage, "If you can't lick them, join them," is illustrated in the subsequent history of this Hellenistic party. Its ideals were perpetuated in the party of the Sadducees, as the ideals of the Hasidim were perpetuated in the party of the Pharisees. These parties are first mentioned during the lifetime of Hyrcanus. Before his death he repudiated the Pharisees and declared himself a Sadducee.

The reign of John Hyrcanus began a policy of territorial expansion including the re-conquest of the coastal cities ceded to Syria during the first years of his reign and the subsequent conquest of Edom, or Idumea.

The coastal cities were the commercial highways of Palestine. From time immemorial the roads of commerce and warfare passed up the Palestinian coastland from Egypt to Syria and Mesopotamia. Without the control of these commercial highways, Hyrcanus knew that Judea would sink into insignificance. As soon as Syrian internal affairs made interference from the north unlikely, Hyrcanus captured the cities and promoted the development of Jewish commerce.

Another ancient trade route passed south of Judea, through Idumea, to Egypt. Hyrcanus conquered this territory and compelled the Idumeans to be circumcised and accept Judaism. This action has been condemned by later Judaism. It even met opposition in his own lifetime. There is something ironical in the thought of a grandson of Mattathias forcing religious conformity on a people conquered by Jewish arms! Many historical parallels may be drawn. The oppressed frequently become the oppressors. That human nature frequently descends to such depths does not lessen the tragedy, however.

Hyrcanus' policy of conquest was supported by the men of wealth and the aristocrats who hoped to grow in power and prestige as a result of new commercial opportunities and larger territories to govern. Some support probably came from extreme nationalists who dreamed of glory and conquest.

The mass of the population, however, could not hope to profit from the policy of territorial expansion. On the contrary, they were alarmed at the growing secularism of the age. The high priesthood had little semblance to a sacred office.

There were practical considerations, too. Wars are expensive — in lives as well as money. The Jew might applaud the conquest of Samaria, whose rival temple on Mt. Gerizim always annoyed him. Perhaps he would even deem the coastal cities a rightful part of his Judean homeland. The annexation of Idumea, however, was something different.

Although there was difference of opinion, and the emergence of rival parties during the reign of Hyrcanus, the unity of the Hasmonean state was not threatened. The borders had been extended on all sides before Hyrcanus died in 104 B.C. Although devout Jews frequently differed with his policies, his personal life was free from suspicion. His devout, Hasidic background bore fruit in a life which could not offend the most meticulous scribe. His children, however, had grown up in a palace and numbered themselves among the aristocrats. Their training was more in Greek than in Hebrew thought, and they looked upon the Pharisees with disdain.

2.   Aristobulus

The death of John Hyrcanus precipitated a dynastic struggle among his children. His eldest son, who preferred his Greek name, Aristobulus, to his Hebrew name, Judah, emerged as the victor. As a typical tyrant, he cast three of his brothers into prison, where two are thought to have starved to death. Another brother was murdered in the palace.

Aristobulus continued the policy of territorial expansion begun by Hyrcanus. In his short reign he pushed his borders north to the territory around Mt. Lebanon, and took to himself the title "King." Drink, disease, and the haunting fear of rebellion brought death after only a one-year reign. There was little mourning among the masses of the Jews.

3.   Alexander Jannaeus

At the time of Aristobulus' death he had but one brother alive in prison. His Hebrew name was Jonathan, and his Greek name, Alexander. History knows him as Alexander Jannaeus.

Any who hoped for a change in policy when Alexander Jannaeus assumed office were bitterly disappointed. The policy of territorial expansion continued. Although not always successful on the battlefield, Jannaeus extended his frontiers along the Philistine coast, toward the frontiers of Egypt and in the Trans-Jordan area. The size of the Jewish state was comparable to that of the glorious days of David and Solomon. It incorporated the whole of Palestine proper, with adjacent areas, from the borders of Egypt to Lake Hulah. Perea in Trans-Jordan was included, as were the Philistine cities of the coastal plain, except Ascalon. The Hasmoneans aspired to become a maritime power. Ships were sculptured on the family tomb near Modein and were depicted on the coins minted by successive Hasmonean rulers.

The territories incorporated into the Hasmonean kingdom were, with some exceptions, quickly Judaized. The Idumeans came to exercise an important place in Jewish national life. Galilee became one of the principal centers of Judaism. The Samaritans, however, resisted assimilation. Cities like Apollonia and Sythopolis, with only a small Jewish element in their population, likewise retained their non-Jewish character.

The rift between the Pharisees and the Hasmonean rulers, first noted in the reign of John Hyrcanus, reached its climax during the days of Alexander Jannaeus. Jannaeus kept the Pharisees in subjection by the use of foreign mercenaries.

Open rebellion broke out at a memorable Feast of Tabernacles when Jannaeus was officiating in the Temple as King-Priest. Showing his contempt for the Pharisees, Jannaeus poured out a water libation at his feet instead of on the altar, as prescribed by Pharisaic ritual. The people in the Temple, enraged at this impious act, pelted Jannaeus with the citrons which they were carrying in honor of the feast. Jannaeus called upon his soldiers to restore order. Hundreds of defenseless people were killed in the process.

The result was open civil war. The Pharisees invited the king of Syria to aid them. War brings strange allies! The descendants of the Hasidim asked the descendants of Antiochus Epiphanes to aid them against the descendants of the Maccabees.

The Syrians came and, aided by the Pharisees, forced Jannaeus into hiding in the Judean hills. The Pharisees did some serious thinking. Fearing that the Syrians would claim Judea as the fruit of victory, and thinking that Alexander Jannaeus and his Sadducean sympathizers were sufficiently punished, thousands of the Pharisees deserted the Syrian army and went over to Jannaeus. The Syrians were defeated by this realignment of forces.

Jannaeus was not content to learn from his near-defeat, however. He instituted a hunt for the leaders of the rebellion, and made a horrible example of those he caught. He gave a banquet to the Sadducean leaders to celebrate his victory. Eight hundred Pharisees were crucified in the presence of his celebrating guests. Alexander Jannaeus thus goes down in history as a tyrant. Compromise between the Pharisees and the Sadducees was rendered impossible. Many students of the Dead Sea Scrolls identify Jannaeus as the Wicked Priest who persecuted the pious leader known as the Teacher of Righteousness.

Tradition suggests that Jannaeus repented on his deathbed. It relates how he instructed his wife, Salome Alexandra, to dismiss his Sadducean advisers and reign with the aid of the Pharisees.

4. Alexandra

Salome Alexandra had been married successively to Aristobulus and Alexander Jannaeus. The widow of two Hasmonean rulers, she succeeded to the throne as queen in her own right. Alexandra was nearly seventy years of age when she began her reign. Being a woman, she could not officiate as High Priest. Her elder son, Hyrcanus, assumed the priesthood, and his brother Aristobulus received the military command. Alexandra's brother, Simeon ben Shetah, was a leader of the Pharisees, a fact which may have disposed Salome Alexandra to seek peace between the opposing factions.

Under Alexandra, the Pharisees had their opportunity to make a constructive contribution to Jewish life. In many areas, particularly that of education, they were eminently successful. Under the presidency of Simeon ben Shetah, the Sanhedrin (the Jewish Council of State) decreed that every young man should be educated. This education was, of course, primarily in the Hebrew Scriptures. The importance of training the young was emphasized in the Old Testament, and the successors of Ezra had stressed the necessity of becoming acquainted with the Sacred Scriptures. Under the leadership of Simeon ben Shetah, a comprehensive system of elementary education was inaugurated, so that the larger villages, towns, and cities of Judea would produce a literate, informed people.

The reign of Alexandra was peaceful in comparison with the years which preceded it. Her son Aristobulus led an expedition against Damascus, which proved futile. A threatened invasion from Armenia was averted by bribes and diplomacy.

Alexandra's reign did not answer her country's problems, however. It did not even heal its wounds. If the Pharisees were happy in their new-found recognition, the Sadducees were resentful of the fact that they were deprived of power. To make matters worse, the Pharisees used their power to seek revenge for the massacre of their leaders by Alexander Jannaeus. Sadducean blood was spilt, and the makings of another civil war were in the air.

The Sadducees found in Aristobulus, the younger son of Jannaeus and Alexandra, the man they would support as Alexandra's successor. He was a soldier, and appealed to that party which dreamed of imperial expansion and worldly power. Hyrcanus, the elder brother and rightful heir, was congenial to the Pharisees. With the death of Alexandra, the partisans of the two sons were ready for a showdown.

5. Hyrcanus II

At the death of Alexandra, her older son Hyrcanus, who had been serving as High Priest, succeeded to the throne as Hyrcanus II. Immediately Aristobulus led an army of Sadducees against Jerusalem. Hyrcanus and the Pharisees had neither enthusiasm for, nor ability in war. Declaring that he never really desired the throne, Hyrcanus surrendered all his honors to Aristobulus who became king and High Priest under the name Aristobulus II.

6. Aristobulus II

By right of conquest, the Judean throne was safely in the hands of Aristobulus II, backed by the Sadducees. Hyrcanus and Aristobulus vowed eternal friendship. Aristobulus' eldest son, Alexander, married Hyrcanus' only daughter, Alexandra. Peace between the brothers was short-lived, however. Hyrcanus found it advisable, or necessary, to flee to Aretas, king of the Nabatean Arabs.

7. Antipater

Antipater, an Idumean by birth, saw in the position of Hyrcanus an opportunity to fulfill his own dream of being a political power in Judea. It was not difficult to persuade Hyrcanus that he had been unjustly deprived of his hereditary rights by his younger brother. The Nabatean Arabs would come to Jerusalem, drive out the usurper, and restore Hyrcanus to his rightful position. Such was the suggestion of Antipater. Hyrcanus agreed. Aretas and his Nabatean Arabs invaded Palestine and besieged Jerusalem. Aristobulus was caught by surprise. He shut himself up in Jerusalem and both sides prepared for a long siege.

8. Enter the Romans

Learning about the quarrel between the brothers, Pompey, who was in the East in the interest of building up the Roman Empire there, took an immediate interest in Jewish politics. Under the guise of a willingness to arbitrate the difficulties, Rome became the force which was to determine the future of Palestine.

14

THE ROMANS TAKE OVER

I. Roman Beginnings

About three decades before Samaria fell to the Assyrians, legend states that Romulus and Remus founded the city of Rome (753 B.C.). Among the nations of antiquity, Rome was a newcomer. The glories of the Sumerians, the Hittites, Mittani, the old Babylonian empire of Hammurabi, and the best periods of Egyptian history had faded centuries before Rome appeared as a city state on the Tiber. During the early years of her existence the mighty Assyrian Empire was defeated by Cyaxeres the Mede and Nabopolassar, the founder of the Neo-Babylonian Empire. Before Rome became a power to be reckoned with, Nabonidus, the last of the Neo-Babylonian kings, was defeated by the armies of Cyrus the Great, and Persia became mistress of the entire East, including Egypt. The son of Philip of Macedon, Alexander the Great, reversed the process of history by invading the East as a missionary for Hellenism and a military conqueror. Alexander's death precipitated the division of the Hellenistic world, which was united again by the diplomacy and the military might of Rome.

Although we are dependent on legend for our accounts of the founding of Rome, its later history is well documented. In the fifth century B.C. the city state of Rome was a thriving republic. By the middle of the third century a series of wars with the Etruscans and other tribes made the whole Italian peninsula subject to Rome. After three wars with the Carthaginians, Rome gained control of the western Mediterranean in 146 B.C. The Carthaginians traced their roots back to the Phoenician city of Tyre, and the wars between Rome and Carthage are known in history as the Punic wars. In 146 B.C. Carthage was completely destroyed by the Roman general,

Scipio Africanus, who put an end to a power which had threatened Rome itself when Hannibal invaded Italy.

Turning toward the east, Rome was able to add to her territories with little opposition. Shortly after the destruction of Carthage, Roman rule was extended over Macedonia, Corinth, and all Achaia. In 133 B.C., Attalus, king of Pergamum, bequeathed his territory to the Romans. The Roman province of Asia was then organized.

2.   Pompey Enters Palestine

In Palestine the strength — both moral and physical — of the Maccabees was fast waning. Following the death of Alexandra, her sons Aristobulus II and Hyrcanus II were fighting for the right of succession. The news of the chaos in Palestine reached Rome. Pompey, the Roman general who had been so successful in bringing Roman power to the East, determined to intervene. Scaurus, one of Pompey's subordinates, decided to support Aristobulus, on the theory that he would be best able to pay the bribe for Roman support which had been offered by each of the contestants.

Pompey personally intervened to get at the root of the quarrel between Aristobulus and Hyrcanus. He observed evidences of the plan of Aristobulus to revolt against Rome. A Roman army besieged Jerusalem. Hyrcanus supported Pompey against his brother. Jerusalem was besieged for three months. Finally the fortifications were breached. Twelve thousand Jews are said to have been slaughtered in the battle which followed. Pompey, with his officers, entered the Holy of Holies in the Temple. This act scandalized the Jews, for none but the High Priest ever had access to the inner court of the Temple. Pompey did not plunder the Temple, however. He left its costly furnishings untouched and permitted the Temple worship to continue. Jerusalem was, in the words of Josephus, "made tributary to the Romans," and the last vestige of Jewish national independence was removed.

With the defeat of Aristobulus, Judea was made a part of the Roman province of Syria. The coastal cities, the district of Samaria, and the non-Jewish cities east of the Jordan were removed from Judea. Hyrcanus was rewarded for his loyalty to Pompey by being named Ethnarch of Judea, including the districts of Galilee, Idumea, and Perea. He was also confirmed in the office of High Priest. A yearly tribute was paid to Rome.

Aristobulus and a number of other captives were taken as prisoners to grace Pompey's triumph in Rome. Enroute to

Rome, Aristobulus' son, Alexander, escaped and attempted to organize a revolt against Hyrcanus. With the aid of the Romans, Hyrcanus was able to meet this challenge to his authority. Alexander was forced to surrender, but his life was spared.

3. The Power of Antipater

During the years of strife between Aristobulus II and Hyrcanus II the Idumean governor Antipater, or Antipas, took a lively interest in the politics of Judea. Antipater was bitterly opposed to Aristobulus, partly through fear and partly because of his friendship for Hyrcanus. It appears that Hyrcanus relied much on Antipater, who became the virtual power behind the throne.

The Jews resented the presence of Antipater almost as much as they resented the fact that they were subject to Rome. Antipater was an Idumean, or Edomite according to Old Testament nomenclature. The Edomites had been the hereditary enemies of the Jews. From the territory south of the Dead Sea they had been pushed northward to the area around Hebron by the Nabatean Arabs. Under John Hyrcanus the Idumeans had been forcibly incorporated into the Jewish nation, and the antipathy continued. Antipater did not let this hinder him from seeking an ever increasing amount of power under Hyrcanus II and his Roman overlords, and from seeking positions of influence for his sons Phasael and Herod.

4. Herod the Great

In the crisis which followed the murder of Julius Caesar, Antipater and his sons showed their loyalty to the new regime of Cassius by zealously collecting tribute. Herod was given the title "Procurator of Judea," with the promise that he would one day be named king. When Anthony defeated Brutus and Cassius at Philippi, Asia fell into the hands of a new Roman regime. Herod, ever an opportunist, quickly changed his loyalties and bribed his way to favor with Anthony.

The Parthians, who occupied a part of the eastern territory of the once mighty Persian Empire, had not been subdued by Rome. In 41 B.C. they attacked and took Jerusalem and made Antigonus, son of Aristobulus II, king and High Priest. Herod, the son of Antipater, who had inherited the throne of Judea at the death of Hyrcanus, was forced to flee to Rome. There he won the favor of Anthony who bestowed upon him the title "King of the Jews," which was to have meaning only after the

Parthians were driven out. The Roman forces helped Herod
in this military operation.

Herod's rule spanned the eventful years of 37 B.C. to 4 B.C.
He is best known as the king who feared the birth of a rival
"King of the Jews," and caused the murder of the infants of
Bethlehem at the time of the birth of Jesus. While that act of
Herod has not been preserved in secular records, his other atroci-
ties are well documented.

Shortly after capturing Jerusalem from the Parthians, Herod
appointed Hananiel of Babylon as High Priest. Herod had married Mariamne, a descendant of the Hasmoneans, thus strengthening his claim to the throne. Her mother, Alexandra, resented
the fact that a non-Hasmonean priest occupied the highest office.
She determined to have Aristobulus, grandson of Hyrcanus II,
as High Priest, and used all of her wiles to accomplish her purpose. Alexandra communicated with Cleopatra of Egypt to influence Anthony to bring pressure on Herod! Her plan was successful. Contrary to Jewish law, Hananiel was removed from
office and Aristobulus was named High Priest.

For a time it looked as though Herod and Alexandra were on
friendly terms. Herod, however, learned of Alexandra's com-
munications with Cleopatra and realized that she could not be
trusted. He insisted that she remain in the palace, and ordered
guards to keep constant watch over her movements. On one occasion she tried to escape to Egypt with her son Aristobulus in
two specially prepared coffins, but one of Herod's servants discovered the plot and prevented the escape.

Aristobulus was a real threat to Herod. As a Jew of priestly
line, he had an advantage which the Idumean, Herod, could not
attain. When the news that Aristobulus had drowned while
bathing reached Herod, he feigned great sorrow. Alexandra was
sure that Aristobulus had been murdered at Herod's instigation.
There is a flaw in Josephus' account of the incident. He records
that Aristobulus "was sent by night to Jericho, and was there
plunged into a pool till he was drowned, by the Gauls, at
Herod's command." The Gauls were not in Herod's service
until five years after Aristobulus' murder.[1] Nevertheless it seems
that Josephus is correct in ascribing to Herod the murder of
Aristobulus.

Alexandra again requested Cleopatra to intervene on her behalf, and was again successful. Anthony commanded Herod to
appear before him to answer for his crime. Herod could not defy

---

1. *Antiquities* xv. 217; *Bell, Jud.* I, 397.

Anthony, so he planned to go to Egypt. First, however, he asked his uncle, Joseph, to look after his affairs during his absence. In the event that Anthony pronounced the death sentence upon Herod, Mariamne, his wife, was to be immediately killed. Herod could not bear the thought of her belonging to anyone else, and he suspected that Anthony had been attracted by her beauty.

When a report reached Jerusalem that Herod had been slain, Alexandra made plans to secure the kingdom for her family. Joseph told Mariamne of the order which Herod had made before leaving for Egypt. Alexandra's plans to secure the kingdom from Anthony, with Mariamne's aid, were frustrated when Herod returned home. The report of his death was untrue. He had explained things to Anthony and had returned with full power.

When Mariamne revealed her knowledge of the order which Herod had given to Joseph, Herod concluded that there had been criminal relations between Joseph and Mariamne. Joseph was put to death with no opportunity to defend himself. Alexandra was "bound" and "kept in custody" because of her part in the affair. For the moment, Mariamne escaped censure. Herod seems to have truly loved her, unwise though he was in his expressions of love.

The next crisis in Herod's life was related to the struggle for power within the Roman Empire. The conflict between Anthony and Octavian for supreme control began in 32 B.C. Herod was the protégé of Anthony and desired to actively support him in his bid for control. Anthony, however, realized his need for a buffer state in the East against the Parthians. Herod did not remain idle, for he had to fight the Nabatean Arabs who were taking advantage of the general unrest. After some hard fighting, Herod overcame the Arab resistance.

Anthony did not fare so well, however. The battle of Actium (September 2, 31 B.C.) ended in defeat for Anthony, and Octavian emerged as the ruler of the Roman world. Herod managed to emerge on the winning side after a meeting with Octavian on the Isle of Rhodes. Josephus tells how Herod boasted of his friendship for Anthony and the help he had given in the fight against Octavian, concluding with the observation that Octavian could observe the kind of person Herod is and the loyalty he would show his benefactors, pledging equal loyalty to Octavian.[2] Octavian confirmed Herod in the kingship of Judea.

After the defeat at Actium, Anthony fled with Cleopatra to

2. *Antiquities* xv. 187-93.

Egypt where the last act of their tragedy was played. The Roman armies reached the environs of Alexandria, and Cleopatra determined to rid herself of Anthony. She barricaded herself in a monument with two of her women and made Anthony think she had committed suicide. Anthony, according to plan, thrust his sword into his body but did not succeed in taking his own life. Cleopatra and her women drew the badly wounded Anthony into the monument. His corpse was found there by the Romans when they broke into the monument. It is suspected that Cleopatra realized that her chances of making terms with the Romans would be enhanced if she could rid herself of Anthony.

Octavian personally entered Alexandria, August 1, 30 B.C. Legend says that Cleopatra tried to charm Octavian with her feminine wiles, only to be repulsed by him. Cleopatra's death remains a mystery. One day she was found dead in her royal robes. The story was circulated that she had had an asp (or two asps) brought to her secretly. Small marks, reportedly discovered on her body, were considered proof that she had committed suicide by allowing herself to be bitten by the snakes.

The death of Cleopatra and the conquest of Egypt by the forces of Octavian strengthened Herod's hand in Palestine. Cleopatra's possessions in Palestine, given to her by Ptolemy, were added to Herod's domain. With other cities deeded to Herod by Octavian, Herod ruled a country equal in size to that which Alexander Jannaeus had ruled.

Successful in politics, Herod's domestic problems were to plague him again. Mariamne, who had been entrusted to a servant, Sohemus, when Herod went to meet Octavian at Rhodes, again learned of a plot to kill her in the event of her husband's death. When she greeted Herod angrily on his return, he ordered Sohemus put to death without trial. Mariamne was tried and condemned to death on the charge of adultery and attempt to poison. Remorse and its aftermath, illness, plagued Herod more effectively than his enemies. Alexandra soon afterward was put to death for a new plot against Herod.

Herod did have the confidence of Octavian, who assumed the name Augustus, but he had to make the best of difficult circumstances in his kingdom. He attempted to gain the good will of the Judeans by remitting a third part of their taxes, but antipathy to him continued. The oath of allegiance to Herod and Caesar was resented by the more religious elements among the

Jews. Herod thought highly of the Essenes, and excused them from taking the oath.

Although Herod's reign was one of trouble, much of it brought on by his own jealousy, there are accomplishments for which he should be given credit. Foremost among these are his buildings. Whole cities were built or rebuilt by Herod: Samaria became Sebaste in honor of Augustus; Straton's Tower became Caesarea, with a harbor protected by a mole and a wall with ten towers; Antipatris, northeast of Joppa; Phasaelis in the Jordan Valley, north of Jericho; and Anthedon, thoroughly renovated, became Agrippeion. Fortresses were built: Herodeion, Alexandreion, Hyrkania, Machaerus, and Masada. The gymnasiums, baths, parks, marketplaces, streets, and other luxuries of a Hellenistic culture were part of his building programs.

In the eighteenth year of his reign (20/19 B.C.), Herod began the work of building, or, more correctly, rebuilding the Temple in Jerusalem. The Temple proper, on which priests and Levites were employed, was finished in a year and a half with no interruption in the daily sacrifices. It took eight more years to complete the courts. The entire structure was arranged in terrace form, with one court higher than the other, and the Temple highest of all. The outer court was open to the gentiles and Jews who were unable to approach closer to the Temple because of ceremonial impurities. A "court of the women" and an inner "court of the Israelites" provided, respectively, for the women and men to approach more closely to the sacred Temple precincts which, of course, were entered only by the officiating priesthood.

Work on the surrounding buildings of the Temple was still going on during the ministry of Jesus (cf. John 2:20). The work was completed during the time of the procurator Albinus (A.D. 62-64), only a few years before the armies of Titus destroyed the city of Jerusalem with its Temple (cf. Matt. 24:2, 15-22, 32-35).

Herod's interest in the Temple was doubtless inspired by his love of grandeur, and his desire to be well received by his Jewish subjects. His personal life was such, however, that his gift of the Temple could not clear his name before the Israelites of his own, or subsequent generations.

The last years of Herod were marked by intrigue and conspiracy. Alexander and Aristobulus, his sons by Mariamne, were educated in Rome. They openly boasted of what they would do to those who had been the enemies of their mother when once they came to power. Antipater, Herod's son by his first wife, Doris, determined to eliminate Alexander and Aristobulus as rival claimants to the throne. Charging that they were plotting against Herod's life, Antipater produced documents which incriminated Alexander and Aristobulus. They were tried, convicted, and strangled to death. Antipater himself was later found guilty of attempting to poison Herod, and given the death sentence. Augustus is reported to have commented, "I'd rather be Herod's hog *(hus)* than his son *(huios)*." Out of deference to Jewish dietary laws, Herod did not kill his hogs.

When it was known that Herod was sick and nearing death, several zealous Pharisees pulled down the golden eagle which Herod had unwisely erected over the great gate of the Temple. Regarding this as a "graven image," the Jews resented its presence. Herod ordered the death of these Jewish leaders, a final act of tyranny which caused his memory to be hated by the Jews.

Herod's death came April 1st, 4 B.C. Cancer of the intestines and dropsy are suggested as its causes. It is said that Herod knew that there would be no mourning when he died, so he ordered the imprisonment and death of a number of the leaders of the Jews that there might be mourning throughout the land. Although this story is probably untrue, Herod left behind him a reputation of infamy. True, he was manipulated by evil people, and was often "more sinned against than sinning," yet he allowed his passions to master him and he must go down in history as one of the world's great failures. That he was jealous even of the infant Jesus shows the extent to which the desire for worldly sovereignty may lead a man astray.

15

THE ORIGIN OF THE JEWISH SECTS

The rise of the Jewish sects is traceable to the impact of Hellenism on the life and culture of the Near East. When the new clashes with the old, violent reactions frequently result. This is particularly true when the new ideology has religious and moral overtones.

Many of the Jews were willing to attempt a synthesis of Greek civilization and Hebrew religion. Jews in Palestine as well as Jews throughout the Hellenistic world, adopted Greek names, subscribed to Greek philosophies, and looked to Greek institutions as the harbingers of cultural progress. The Jews in Palestine were generally more conservative than their Greek-speaking cousins in Alexandria and the other great Hellenistic centers, but they were not unaffected. We may assume that these Jews felt that their loyalty to the faith of their fathers was in no way impaired by making peace with the new attitudes which Alexander and his successors had advocated.

Other Jews reacted violently against the Hellenizers. They saw Hellenism as a way of life which was opposed to that prescribed in their Torah. The immodesty of the Greek gymnasium and the neglect of Jewish religious rites by the Hellenistically minded younger generation seemed to indicate trouble. As idolatry had been the besetting sin of Israel before the exile, so Hellenism was regarded as the new temptation to unfaithfulness.

The Jews who reacted against Hellenism are known as the Hasidim (Chasidim) or Assidians. They were, by definition, the party of "the pious." As the Sadducees of New Testament times continued the basic ideology of the earlier Hellenizers, so the Pharisees and the Essenes sought to preserve the basic tenets of the Hasidim. The law of God was basic in Hasidic thought. They were willing to suffer martyrdom rather than transgress its precepts. They supported the sons of Mattathias in the early days of the Maccabean revolt, but they left the Hasmoneans as soon as their religious liberties had been won from the Seleucids. Freedom to obey the law was to them an adequate goal, and political independence was quite unnecessary.

1. The Pharisees

The party of the Pharisees is first mentioned by name during the reign of John Hyrcanus (134-104 B.C.). According to Josephus, Hyrcanus expressed his friendship to his fellow Pharisees by inviting them to a feast, during which he urged any who observed anything unbecoming in his conduct to correct him. A Pharisee replied that, if Hyrcanus really wanted to be righteous, he should surrender the office of High Priest and be content with his position as civil ruler. The Pharisee suggested that Hyrcanus' mother had been a captive in the days of Antiochus which, it would be presumed, would have involved her in immorality.

Hyrcanus was enraged at this suggestion, and the other Pharisees seemed to resent the charge made by one of their number. Josephus tells us that a Sadducee took advantage of the embarrassment of the situation by suggesting that Hyrcanus ask the Pharisees to suggest a suitable punishment for their offending member. In this way the attitude of the Pharisees as a sect would become apparent. When the Pharisees suggested "a moderate punishment of stripes" rather than the death penalty, Hyrcanus felt that the Pharisees were really opposed to him, and he espoused the cause of the Sadducees.

To what extent the story is to be regarded as sober history would be difficult to determine, but it suggests the antagonism between the Pharisees and Sadducees as early as the reign of Hyrcanus. It is clear that the Pharisees resented the combination of high priesthood and civil authority in the successors of the Maccabees. It has been suggested that the outspoken Pharisee who incurred the wrath of Hyrcanus may have left the more moderate Pharisees to become the founder of the Essenes. This is, of course, only a conjecture.

The word "Pharisee" means "separated ones." Although some have suggested that the separation was from the common people, it is more probable that the Pharisees were so named because of their zeal for the law which involved separation from the influences of Hellenism. In this sense they were the heirs of the Hasidim. Josephus says that the Pharisees "appear more religious than others, and seem to interpret the laws more accurately."

The laws regarding ceremonial purity were punctiliously observed by members of the Pharisaic brotherhood. No items of food or drink were to be purchased from a "sinner," for fear of ceremonial defilement. For the same reason, a Pharisee might not eat in the house of a "sinner," although he might entertain the "sinner" in his own house. When this was done, however, the Pharisee was required to provide the "sinner" with clothes to wear, for the "sinner's" own clothes might be ceremonially impure.

The particular domain of the Pharisees in pre-Christian Judaism was the synagogue. The synagogue seems to have had its origin in the Babylonian captivity when the Jews were prevented from participating in the sacrificial offerings which could be offered only in the Jerusalem Temple. Prayer and the reading of Scripture, however, were not subject to limitations of geography. Wherever ten Jewish families settled, a synagogue could be formed, according to later usage. After the return from exile, the synagogue was retained as the place of non-sacrificial worship in Israel, as it is to this day. The Sadducees gained control of the Temple ritual during the period that the Hasmoneans ruled, and down to New Testament times, but the scribes and Pharisees maintained the synagogue as the center of worship and instruction.

In a sincere desire to make the law workable within the changing culture of the Greco-Roman world, the Pharisaic scribes developed the system of oral tradition which proved such a burden to Judaism during the time of Christ.

Beginning with Scripture itself, the Pharisees quoted the "case decisions" of famous rabbis who had been consulted concerning the application of Scripture to individual problems. If the revered exegetes of Scripture (the *hakamim*, or sages) had expressed an opinion concerning the application or meaning of Scripture, this was given due consideration. Thus the observant Jew was frequently faced with conflicting viewpoints on the nature of correct Sabbath observance, the application of dietary rules to new articles of food, and the multitude of problems with which the legalistic mind was burdened.

During the first century before Christ, two influential Pharisaic teachers gave their names to the two historic schools of legal thought among the Pharisees. Hillel was the more moderate of the two in his legal interpretations. He was known for his regard for the poor and was willing to accept Roman rule as compatible with Jewish orthodoxy. Shammai, on the other hand, was more strict in his interpretation, and was bitterly opposed to the Romans. This viewpoint ultimately found expression in the Zealots, whose resistance to the Romans brought on the destruction of Jerusalem in A.D. 70. The Talmud preserves the record of 316 controversies between the schools of Hillel and Shammai.

The attempts at applying the Law to new situations were rejected by the Sadducees who restricted their concept of authority to the Torah, or Mosiac Law. The medieval Jewish sect of Karaites similarly rejected the rabbinical interpretations of Scripture and appealed for a return to the Bible itself as alone valid as the standard of faith. To the Pharisees, however, tradition was not simply a commentary upon the Law, but was ultimately raised to the level of Scripture itself. To justify this attitude it was stated that the "oral law" was given by God to Moses at Mt. Sinai, along with the "written Law" or the Torah (*Pirke Aboth.* 1:1). The ultimate in this development is reached when the Mishna states that the oral law must be observed with greater stringency than the written Law, because statutory law (i.e., oral tradition) affects the life of the ordinary man more intimately than the more remote constitutional Law (the written Torah) (M. Sanhedrin 10:3).

In addition to the charge that traditions had largely made void the intent of the Law, the New Testament makes it clear that the mentality of Pharisaism involved little more than a concern for the minutia of the Law during the time of Christ. Like many worthy movements, the early piety of those who had separated themselves from impurity at great cost was exchanged for an attitude of pride in the observance of legal precepts. The Pharisee scrupulously tithed even his wild herbs (Matt. 23:23; Luke 11:42), but he did not hesitate to oppress the weak and needy at the same time. (cf. Matt. 23:14). Fasting, ceremonial ablutions, Sabbath observance were all proper in their place, according to Jesus, but they were not enough. They must be accompanied by evidence of a heart that truly loved the Lord. Conspicuous tassels and phylacteries (Matt. 23:5) and long public prayers (Mark 12:40, Luke 20:47) gave a degree of sanctity to the Pharisees in the eyes of the people, but this must not be confused with true piety before God. If the Pharisees desire to be seen of men, "they have their reward." This must not be confused with a life lived to the glory of God, however.

In men like Nicodemus, Joseph of Arimathea, Gamaliel, and Saul of Tarsus we meet some of the nobler souls of the Pharisaic tradition in the New Testament. To Saul of Tarsus who became Paul the apostle, the Pharisee represented the epitome of orthodoxy, "the most straitest sect of our religion" (Acts 26:5). The degeneracy of Pharisaism serves as a warning to those who take a stand for separation from evil. Self-complacency and spiritual pride are temptations to which the pious are particularly susceptible.

2. The Sadducees

Although the Pharisees and Sadducees are frequently denounced together in the New Testament, they had little in common save their antagonism to Jesus.

The Sadducees were the party of the Jerusalem aristocracy and the high priesthood. They had made their peace with the political rulers and had attained positions of wealth and influence. Temple administration and ritual was their specific responsibility. In the later Hasmonean period and the Roman period which followed it, the high priesthood had become a political football so that the religious interests of the office tended to be pushed into the background. The Sadducees held themselves aloof from the masses and were unpopular with them.

Theologically the Sadducees must be described with a series of negatives. They did not accept the oral law which developed under the Pharisees, and seem to have limited their canon to the Torah, or Pentateuch. They did not believe in resurrection, spirits, or angels (cf. Mark 12:18; Luke 20:27; Acts 23:8). They left no positive religious or theological system.

The Pharisees welcomed and sought proselytes (cf. Matt. 23:15), but the Sadducean party was closed. None but the members of the High Priestly and aristocratic families of Jerusalem could be Sadducees. With the destruction of the Jerusalem Temple in A.D. 70, the Sadducees came to an end. Modern Judaism traces its roots to the party of the Pharisees.

3. The Essenes

The Essenes and the Pharisees both continued the testimony of Hasidim. The Pharisees maintained their strict orthodoxy within the framework of historical Judaism. Their separation was from defilement, but not from institutional Judaism as such. Even though the Temple worship was conducted by the

Sadducees, the Pharisees esteemed it a basic part of their religious inheritance. The Pharisee might hold himself aloof from "sinners," but he lived among them and coveted their esteem.

A more extreme reaction against the influences which tend to corrupt Jewish life was taken by the sect which the ancient writers Philo, Josephus, and Pliny call the Essenes. They seem to have lived for the most part in monastic communities, such as that with headquarters at Qumran, from which the Dead Sea scrolls have come.

In seeking to explain Judaism to the Greek-speaking world, Josephus spoke of three "philosophies" — Pharisees, Sadducees, and Essenes. The term "Essene" seems to have had quite an elastic usage, however, including various groups of monastically minded Jews who differed among themselves in certain of their practices. Pliny says that the Essenes avoided women and did not marry, but Josephus speaks of an order of marrying Essenes. The excavations of the cemetery at Qumran similarly reveal that women were a part of the Qumran community.

The ancient writers deal in a sympathetic way with the Essenes. The life of the Essene was one of rigor and simplicity. Devotion and religious study occupied an important place in the community. Scripture and other religious books were studied and copied by members of the Essene community. Each Essene was required to perform manual labor to make the community self-supporting. Community of goods was practiced in the Essene communities, and strict discipline was enforced by an overseer. Those groups which renounced marriage adopted boys at an early age in order to inculcate and perpetuate the ideals of Essenism. Slavery and war were repudiated.

The Essenes accepted proselytes, but the novice was required to go through a period of strict probation before he could become a full-fledged member. Numerically the Essenes were never large. Philo says that there were four thousand of them. Pliny says that they were settled north of En Gedi, an apparent reference to Qumran, northwest of the Dead Sea. That there were other settlements is clear, for we are told that all members of the sect were welcome in any of the Essene colonies.

Although it has been suggested that the Essenes are an offshoot of Pharisaism, dating back to the time of John Hyrcanus, nothing certain is known of their early history. Considering themselves the true Israel, they trace their history back to the beginnings. Philo states that Moses instituted the order, and Josephus says that they existed "ever since the ancient time of the fathers." Pliny agrees that their history covers "thousands of ages." It is certain that Essenes existed for two centuries before the Christian era and that they lived at first among the Jewish communities. When they ultimately withdrew, many seem to have settled at Qumran, others living in scattered communities throughout Syria and Palestine.

The question of foreign influences on Essene thinking has been the subject of much scholarly debate. While some maintain that the Essenes are a purely indigenous growth within Judaism, others suggest that they were influenced from without — either from western Greek ideas, or from eastern Syrian or Persian concepts.

Josephus tells us that the Essenes believed in immortality but rejected the doctrine of bodily resurrection. This seems to be related to the philosophical concept of the evil of matter. The body is material, and if matter is evil, then salvation comes by escaping the body, and a bodily resurrection would be undesirable. Enforced celibacy fits into the same concept, which is contrary to the teaching of both Old Testament and New Testament Scripture. Early Christian theology was confronted with a similar heresy when the Docetists claimed that Jesus did not really have a body. Since they believed that matter is evil, they could not conceive of the Son of God as having a real body.

Although the Essenes either discouraged or forbade marriage, the Pharisees expected every man to take a wife at the age of eighteen. In this respect they were closer to the ideals of Biblical religion than were the Essenes.

While the Pharisees took part in the Temple services, even though they were unhappy at the position of the unorthodox Sadducees, the Essenes regarded themselves as the only true, or pure, Israel and refused to co-operate with what they believed to be the corrupt religious observances at the Jerusalem Temple. The carefully regulated life at the Essene center seems to have served as a substitute for the Temple in the eyes of the Essenes.

The strictness of Essene discipline and the rigidity with which the law was enforced are stressed by all who write about them. Josephus says that they were stricter than all Jews in abstaining from work on the Sabbath day (*Wars*. II. vii. 9). A passage in the Damascus Document, related to the Dead Sea Scrolls, says that it is unlawful to lift an animal out of a pit on the Sabbath day. Such a view was considered extreme even by the legalistic Pharisees (cf. Matt. 12:11).

The absence of references to the Essenes in the New Testa-

ment has led many writers to conclude that Jesus and the early
church were Essene in sympathies, if not in origin. Renan called
Christianity "an Essenism which succeeded on a broad scale,"
and E. Schure held that Jesus had been initiated into the secret
doctrines of the Essenes.

Although the Essenes are not mentioned in the New Testament, they are also absent from the Jewish Talmud. The Pharisees and the Sadducees were the groups with which Jesus had immediate contact, and it is to be expected that they would be the
ones who were the subjects of His discourses.

The teaching and practice of Jesus is diametrically opposed
to the legalism and asceticism of the Essenes. Although the Essenes considered that contact with a member of their own group
of a lower order than themselves was ceremonially defiling, Jesus
did not hesitate to eat and drink with "publicans and sinners"
(Matt. 11:9, Luke 7:34). Although obedient to the Mosaic Law,
Jesus had no sympathy with those who made of the Law a burden instead of a blessing. The Sabbath was made for man, and
Jesus insisted that it was lawful to do good on the Sabbath day
(Matt. 12:1-12; Mark 2:23-36; Luke 6:6-11; 14:1-6).

Contrary to the Essene idea that matter is evil, Jesus insisted
that it is from within, out of the heart of man, that evil comes.
His first miracle was performed at a wedding (John 2:1).

Jesus denounced abuses in the Temple, and prophesied its
destruction, but he did not repudiate the Temple services. He
came to Jerusalem for the great feasts of His people, and after
His resurrection we find Peter and John going to the Temple
at the hour of prayer (Acts 3:1).

Asceticism and monasticism early gained entrance to the
Christian church. Christianity in its earliest period, however,
cannot be called an ascetic movement. The ministry of Jesus
was largely to the "common people" who "heard Him gladly"
(Mark 12:37), when the self-righteous despised both Him and
them. He was called "a winebibber" and "a friend of publicans
and sinners"—names which would scandalize Pharisee, Sadducee,
and Essene alike (Luke 7:34).

4. The Zadokites

Since the publication in 1910 by Solomon Schechter of *Fragments of a Zadokite Work*—discovered in 1896 in the genizeh, or
storage room for worn out manuscripts, of a Cairo synagogue—
the term "zadokite" has entered the discussion of sectarian Judaism. The term "zadokite" appears to be related to the word

"Sadducee," but the two groups had different historical developments. Some have suggested that a group of spiritually minded priests, alarmed at the drift toward worldliness of early second century B.C. Sadduceeism, separated from it and formed the nucleus for the new group of "sons of Zadok." Whether this movement found spiritual affinity with a group like the Essenes, or whether a new beginning is to be posited for the group at this time is not clear.

The Zadokite Work speaks of a group which was compelled to migrate to Damascus where, under the leadership of a man called "the star" (cf. Num. 24:17), they entered into a New Covenant (cf. Jer. 31:31). A prominent leader of the sect, who may have been the founder, is the Teacher of Righteousness mentioned in the Zadokite work and the Qumran scrolls.

Scholars are agreed that the Zadokite work is related to the Qumran manuscripts. Style, vocabulary, and historical allusions first suggested a relationship. The discovery of copies of the Zadokite work in Cave 6, Qumran, removed any doubts. The history of the Qumran community and its relationship to known groups of pre-Christian Jews is still obscure.

The Zadokite work speaks of a migration to Damascus by the group of which the document speaks. The circumstances of this migration are not given in sufficient detail to warrant a positive statement of date. It has been thought that the removal of Onias III from his office as High Priest in the days of Antiochus Epiphanes was the occasion for the flight of the Zadokites to Damascus. Charles Fritsch in *The Qumran Community* suggests that the sojourn took place during the reign of Herod the Great (37 B.C. to 4 B.C.). Archaeological evidence indicates that the Qumran community center was unoccupied at that time, and Fritsch considered this the key to the date of the sojourn in Damascus. This gives rise to several questions: "Did the Zadokites leave Jerusalem around 175 B.C., sojourn for a time in Damascus, and then settle at Qumran? Did they go from Jerusalem to Qumran, then to Damascus during the reign of Herod, and then return to Qumran? Did the Damascus Covenanters, as the Zadokites are called, join forces with another group such as the Essenes?"

A Jewish scholar, Rabinowitz, has suggested that the withdrawal from Judea to Damascus is but another way of describing the Babylonian captivity. The faithful in Israel are thus thought of as learning lessons of loyalty to the Lord "beyond Damascus." Although this view would eliminate certain historical problems, the Zadokite Work does appear to discuss a historical migration to Damascus in days following the return from Babylonian exile.

Present knowledge seems to indicate that a group of priests, "sons of Zaddok," started a movement to which lay members were attracted. In Qumran the priestly prerogatives are jealously guarded. The name Zadokite was applied to the movement because of its stress on its own priestly legitimacy *vis-a-vis* the Jerusalem priesthood. The latter was corrupt in the eyes of the Zadokites. If this reconstruction is correct it would seem that the Qumran community included those who are called the Zadokites. Since the term Essene seems to have been a rather general term assigned to various ascetic groups within pre-Christian Judaism, it seems probable that this group of Zadokites was identified as Essene by Philo, Pliny, and Josephus. Since the historical origins of both Zadokite and Essene groups are still matters of conjecture, we cannot state which group existed first. That there were affinities, however, seems clear.

5. Zealots

Roman rule was not popular with the majority of Jews. To the Pharisees, Roman overlordship was a punishment visited upon Israel because of its sins. It was to be accepted with humility, in prayerful anticipation of the day when God would remove the horrible Roman yoke.

A more extreme attitude was taken by the party known from the writings of Josephus as the Zealots. They first appeared in Galilee under the leadership of Judas the son of Ezekias during the early years of Roman rule. They refused to pay taxes and considered it a sin to acknowledge loyalty to Caesar. God alone was to be reckoned as king of Israel!

The Pharisee, Gamaliel, mistakenly regarded Peter and the apostles as Zealot leaders. He urged that no action be taken against them, believing that if the movement they represented were not of God it would come to naught, as in the case of Theudas and Judas of Galilee. (Acts 5:35-39). The Galilean origin of most of the disciples and the fact that one of them was named Simon Zelotes (Simon, the Zealot) would make such a misunderstanding possible.

Ultimately the Zealots succeeded in winning the bulk of the people to their side. Their continual defiance of Rome brought on the destruction of Jerusalem in A.D. 70.

16

RISE OF THE APOCALYPTIC LITERATURE

During the last two centuries of this period and the first century of the Christian era, a species of literature developed among the Jews which is termed apocalyptic. An apocalypse is an unveiling. The last book of the Bible bears that name. This type of writing is also found in various portions of the Old Testament prophetic books, including Isaiah, Ezekiel (38-39), Daniel, Joel, and Zechariah (12-14).

The chief noncanonical apocalyptic books are the writings ascribed to Enoch and Baruch, the Testament of the Twelve Patriarchs, and IV Ezra. They form a part of the body of ancient literature which is termed pseudepigraphal because of the fact that many of these writings were issued under an assumed name.

The apocalyptic portions of the Bible are actually a species of Biblical prophecy. They are a part of the "divers manners" (Heb. 1:1) used in the proclamation of religious truth by Israel's prophets.

During the two centuries before Christ, when the Jew was conscious of the fact that prophecy had ceased, and that the canon of Scripture was closed, he looked for no new spokesman to declare divine truth with authority — at least until the Messiah should come. Thinkers, however, felt that they had a message for their generation. Sometimes these messages contained words and thoughts which had been popularly ascribed to some ancient worthy. In order to give a production the sanctity of age, and thus to insure a wide audience, the apocalypses of the two pre-Christian centuries were pseudepigraphal. The name of some ancient man of God, like Enoch, was assigned as the author of the writing. The writers doubtless believed that they were writing in the spirit of the earlier patriarch, and much of the material which they used was really old. We should not lightly charge these writers with "pious fraud," although we cannot accept the names assigned to their writings at face value.

Apocalyptic literature was both a message of comfort in days of trouble and an effort to show how God had purposed to bring victory to His people, although they were in the midst of an apparently hopeless situation. The persecutions of Antiochus Epiphanes threatened the very existence of Israel as a people. It was in the consciousness of the sovereign purposes of God that Israel took hope.

The Old Testament prophets were largely preachers, delivering the Word of God by word of mouth to their generation. The apocalyptists wrote their messages. Their writings made frequent use of imagery. In this way they avoided possible reprisals from powerful individuals or groups attacked. Also they secured an impressive air of mystery which helped to reinforce the message.

Students of apocalyptic literature, both Biblical and non-canonical, note a constancy in the imagery. Nations are beasts which come out of the sea (Dan. 7:3; II Esdras 11:1; Rev. 13:1). There are seven heavens (Testament of the Twelve Patriarchs —Levi, iii; Ascension of Isaiah, vii-x). Frequent references are made to "horns," "heads," "watchers," and "the seven angels." In general, men are described as animals, nations as beasts, the Jews as sheep or cattle, and their leaders as rams or bulls.

The apocalyptic literature of the two centuries before Christ adapted the ideas and, in part, the imagery of the earlier prophetic literature to the needs of a new generation. An air of mystery surrounds many of these writings. They deal with the purposes of God, the "secrets" of heaven which are not known to the uninitiated. The knowledge of the divine will comes through vision or dream. The message is usually given in the first person. If Israel's prophet claimed direct revelation from God Himself, the apocalyptic writer claims to receive divine revelation mediately through an angel. The prophets had much to say about the present, but the chief concern of the apocalyptist was the future. The final consummation was regarded as imminent.

The coming Messiah is a recurrent theme for the apocalyptist. This concept finds its roots in the Old Testament. Nathan had spoken of the continuation and idealization of the Davidic line (II Sam. 7:12 ff. cf. Ps. 89). The Perfect Prince of the Apocalyptists was a scion of the house of David. The Psalms of Solomon (17:21 ff.) contain a prayer for a restored Davidic prince who will overthrow the Romans. References to a Messiah, or "Anointed One," from other lines also appear. The Testament of Reuben (6:7 ff.) speaks of a Messiah from the line of Levi, and the Damascus Zadokite fragments speak of a Messiah from Aaron (9:10). In the Similitude of Enoch, written before 63 B.C., the Messiah is called "The Anointed One," "The Righteous One," "The Elect," and "The Son of Man" (37-71). The latter title, so familiar to the reader of the New Testament Gospels, is apparently derived from Daniel 7:13. The apocalyptists frequently speak of the Messiah as the great Judge who will come in the clouds of heaven to punish the wicked and reward the righteous.

The concept of the Kingdom of God is the climax of Apocalyptic literature. Sometimes this is presented as reserved for the Jews, or the righteous Jews only. Other writers envision the Kingdom of God as including true worshipers of God from every nation.

The Kingdom of God in some writers is a period of divine rule on earth. This rule may last four hundred years, or one hundred years, or it may be eternal. If this Kingdom of God is temporary, it is followed by an eternal heavenly existence.

To those who look for a Kingdom of God in this world, the end of the present age means the end of evil in the world. The future age is earthly but not evil. Some, however, insist that the present world is inherently evil. They expect the world to be destroyed, or miraculously changed. The future age is then the heavenly world.

The glories of the Kingdom of God are described in bold language. The earth will be so fruitful that a single vine will bear 10,000 branches, each branch 10,000 twigs, each twig 10,000 shoots, each shoot 10,000 clusters, each cluster 10,000 grapes, and each grape will produce 225 gallons of wine!

To what extent were the apocalyptists influenced by outside sources? It is frequently suggested that Persian influences, particularly in angelology and the dualistic conflicts between light and darkness, account in large measure for the nature of apocalyptic. Greek and Egyptian contacts are also suggested. While the Apocalyptic writers certainly assimilated material from the various cultures which surrounded them, there is no evidence of direct borrowing. It is best to see in the apocalyptic literature an echo of the prophetic writings, given shape by the sufferings under Antiochus Epiphanes. The Christian sees in the Messianic hope expressed in the literature of the first two pre-Christian centuries a providential preparation for the advent of Christ. Behind the extravagant symbolism, exaggerated nationalism, and laborious numerical calculations, he sees a confidence in the ultimate accomplishment of the divine purposes, and the advent of a righteous "son of David" through whom the purposes of God will be realized.

EPILOGUE

In the days of Herod the Great, in an obscure corner of the Roman Empire, in the city which had been the birthplace of King David a millennium earlier, Jesus the Messiah was born. History took little note of his life. Only a few devoted disciples openly espoused his cause. The religious leaders attributed the miracles He performed to Beelzebub, the Prince of the Devils. To the Roman officials he was an insurrectionist; to the Jews, a blasphemer. In the hour of his trial, his disciples forsook Him and fled. He was crucified as a malefactor, between two thieves.

Yet His life and His death introduce a new age. From apparent defeat came the triumph of victory. The death of the cross is heralded as the divinely provided atonement for sin. The resurrection brings the assurance of life everlasting.

CHRONOLOGY

Persian Period

Date B.C.

612	Nineveh destroyed by Medes and Babylonians.
587	Jerusalem destroyed by Nebuchadnezzar.
559	Cyrus inherits kingdom of Anshan, tributary to the Medes.
549	Cyrus of Anshan conquers Astyages, the Mede.
539	Babylon falls to Cyrus. End of Neo-Babylonian Empire.
530-522	Cambyses succeeds Cyrus. Conquest of Egypt.
522-486	Darius I ruler of the Persian Empire.
515	Completion of Second Temple in Jerusalem.
486-465	Xerxes I attempts the conquest of Greece. Time of Esther.
480	Greek naval victory at Salamis. Xerxes flees.
464-424	Artaxerxes I rules Persia. Age of Nehemiah.

The Hellenistic Period

334-323	Alexander the Great conquers the East.
330	Macedonian conquest of Palestine.
311	Seleucus conquers Babylon. Beginning of the Seleucid dynasty.
223-187	Antiochus (III) the Great, Seleucid ruler of Syria.
202	Rome defeats Carthage at Zama.
198	Antiochus III defeats Egypt, gains control of Palestine.
175-163	Antiochus (IV) Epiphanes rules Syria-Palestine. Proscribes Judaism. Persecution of the orthodox Jews.
168	Battle of Pydna. Romans defeat the Macedonians.
167	Mattathias and his sons rebel against the Syrians. Beginning of the Maccabean Revolt.
166-160	Leadership of Judas Maccabaeus.
160-142	Jonathan, High Priest.
146	Scipio Africanus destroys Carthage. Rome controls western Mediterranean.
142-135	Simon, High Priest.
134-104	John Hyrcanus, son of Simon, High Priest and King.
103	Aristobulus.
102-76	Alexander Jannaeus.
75-67	Salome Alexandra ruler; Hyrcanus II High Priest.
66-63	Aristobulus II. Dynastic battle with Hyrcanus II.
63	Pompey invades Palestine. Roman rule begins.
63-40	Hyrcanus II rules, subject to Rome. Antipater exercises increasing power.
40-37	Parthians conquer Jerusalem. Establish Aristobulus II as High Priest and King.
37-4	Herod the Great, son of Antipater, rules as king, subject to Rome.
31	Battle of Actium. Octavian emerges as ruler of the Roman world.

BIBLIOGRAPHY

PRIMARY SOURCE MATERIAL

For annals of Neo-Babylonian and Persian kings, consult Pritchard, J. B., ed., *Ancient Near Eastern Texts Relating to the Old Testament* (Princeton, 1955).

The writings of the Egyptian historian, Manetho, have been edited by W. G. Waddell. They appear in Loeb Classical Library volume 350.

The histories of Herodotus of Halicarnassus have been edited by A. D. Godley. They appear as Loeb Classical Library volumes 117, 118, 119, and 120. A popular translation by Aubrey de Selincourt appears as L34 in the Penguin Classics Series.

The histories of Polybius have been edited by W. R. Paton. They appear as Loeb Classical Library volumes 128, 137, 138, 159, 160, and 161.

The writings of Flavius Josephus have been edited by H. St. J. Thackeray and Ralph Marcus. *The Antiquities of the Jews* appear in the Loeb Classical Library volumes 242, 281, 326, and 365. *The Jewish War* appears in Loeb volumes 203 and 210. *The Life* and *Against Apion* appear as Loeb volume 186.

Jewish Apocryphal and Pseudepigraphal writings were edited by R. H. Charles in conjunction with many scholars in a monumental, two volume work, *The Apocrypha and Pseudepigrapha of the Old Testament* (Oxford, 1913). The Revised Standard Version *Apocrypha* was published by Thomas Nelson and Sons, 1957. A series of individual volumes is in course of publication by Dropsie College and Harper and Brothers. Sidney Tedesche and Solomon Zeitlin have collaborated on the volumes on First and Second Maccabees (1950 and 1954, respectively). Moses Hadas has edited and translated the Third and Fourth Books of Maccabees (1953) and the Letter of Aristeas (1951). Joseph Reider has edited and translated The Book of Wisdom (1957).

The Behistun Inscription of Darius is readily available in *The Greek Historians*, Francis R. B. Godolphin, ed. (Random House, 1942), Volume 2, pp. 623-632.

A translation of the non-Biblical texts from Qumran is available in *The Dead Sea Scriptures* by Theodore H. Gaster (Doubleday, 1957).

The Zadokite Documents have been edited and translated by Chaim Rabin in *The Zadokite Documents* (Oxford, 1954).

SUGGESTIONS FOR FURTHER READING

General

Fairweather, William, *The Background of the Gospels* (T. & T. Clark, 1908).

Oesterley, W. O. E., and Robinson, T. H., *A History of Israel* (Oxford, 1932,) 2 vols.

Snaith, Norman H., *The Jews from Cyrus to Herod* (Abingdon, n.d.)

The pertinent sections of *The Cambridge Ancient History*.

Persia

Girshman, R., *Iran* (Pelican, 1954).

Olmstead, A. T., *The History of the Persian Empire* (Chicago, 1948).

Rogers, Robert William, *A History of Ancient Persia* (Chas. Scribner's Sons, 1929).

Greece

Bury, J. B., *History of Greece to the Death of Alexander the Great* (Macmillan, 1922).

Carey, Max, *A History of the Greek World from 323 to 146 B.C.* (Macmillan, 1952).

Kirto, H. D. F., *The Greeks* (Pelican, 1956).

Oesterley, W. O. E., *The Jews and Judaism during the Greek Period* (Macmillan, 1941).

Hellenism

Bentwich, Norman, *Hellenism* (Jewish Publication Society, 1919).

Bottsford, G. W., and Sihler, E. G., *Hellenic Civilization* (Columbia, 1950).

Marcus, Ralph, "The Hellenistic Age" in *Great Ages and Ideas of the Jewish People,* edited by Leo W. Schwarz (Random House, 1956).

Wolfson, Harry A., *Philo* (Harvard, 1948), 2 vols.

Maccabees and Hasmoneans

Bevan, E. R., *Jerusalem under the High Priests* (Arnold, 1904).

Bickerman, Elias, *The Maccabees* (Schocken, 1947).

Riggs, J. S. *A History of the Jewish People: Maccabean and Roman Periods* (Chas. Scribner's Sons, 1908).

Romans

Barrow, R. H., *The Romans* (Pelican, 1949).

Moore, George Foot, *Judaism in the First Centuries of the Christian Era* (Harvard, 1927), 2 vols.

Perowne, Stewart, *The Life and Times of Herod the Great* (Hodder and Stoughton, 1957).

INDEX